D0492629

home
baking
cookbook

Consultant editor
Jacqueline Bellefontaine

Love Food ® is an imprint of Parragon Books Ltd

Parragon
Queen Street House
4 Queen Street
Bath BA1 1HE, UK

Copyright © Parragon Books Ltd 2006

Love Food ® and the accompanying heart device is a trade mark of Parragon Books Ltd

ISBN: 978-1-4075-5454-9

Printed in China

Created and produced by The Bridgewater Book Company Ltd
Commissioned photography: Clive Bozzard-Hill
Home Economist: Sandra Baddeley

Picture acknowledgements
Jupiterimages Corporation: page 32 (top) and 33.
Getty Images: title page.

Notes for the Reader

This book uses both metric and imperial measurements. Follow the same
units of measurement throughout; do not mix metric and imperial. All spoon
measurements are level: teaspoons are assumed to be 5 ml, and tablespoons are
assumed to be 15 ml. Unless otherwise stated, milk is assumed to be
semi-skimmed and eggs are medium.

Nut allergies
Some recipes contain nuts. If you or your children are allergic to nuts you should
avoid contact with nuts and any products containing nuts.

CONTENTS

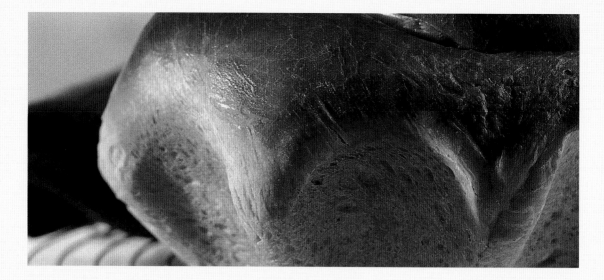

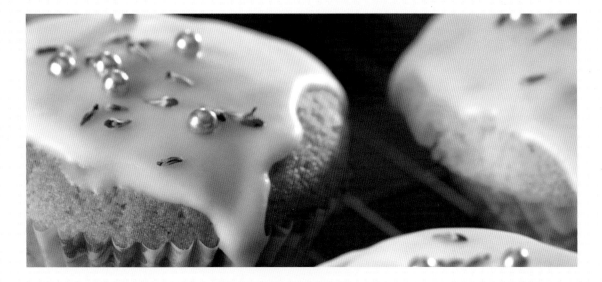

introduction

This book could not begin without an introduction to the basic principles of baking. On the following pages you will find all the information you need to bake cakes, pastry and biscuits with great success. You will be guided through the fundamentals of cake baking from greasing and lining the tin, to cake-making methods, and will be able to answer that all-important question, 'Is it cooked?'

Discover the rules of great pastry, tips for fabulous tasting biscuits and all there is to know about yeast. As if that were not enough to set you on the path to baking bliss, an indispensable 'What went wrong?' guide will clear up any baking misdemeanours, so that you can be assured of perfect results each time you bake.

INTRODUCTION

Few other areas of home cooking are greeted with the same enthusiasm as baking, not just by home bakers themselves, but also by those who are lucky enough to be on the receiving end of home baking. Be they crisp, mouthwatering biscuits, freshly baked bread or satisfying and comforting cakes, nothing quite beats the quality of home-baked goods. Everybody loves the flavour of cakes and buns still warm from the oven, and the aroma of freshly cooked breads is one of life's great delights.

However, many people are put off baking because they think it is difficult or too time-consuming. That is, happily, not the reality. Fabulous baked cakes can actually be mixed in just a few minutes, with only a modicum of skill needed, and can be lifted fresh from the oven in less than 30 minutes. A basic loaf of bread may take a little longer to produce, but often will not demand a great deal of active preparation time from the cook. Of course, some baking requires more time and skill, but the joy of the *Home Baking Cookbook* is that there is something for everyone. Whether you want to produce a quick cake for tea or spend time creating an elaborate gateau that really challenges your baking skills, you will find the ideal recipe in this comprehensive baking book. Novices who need to be guided step by step through the recipes and more accomplished cooks alike will soon discover that the rewards of baking outweigh the effort involved, especially when it comes to other people's unfailing appreciation of the results of your labours. After all, baking is meant to be a sharing, uplifting experience!

While to become an outstanding home baker does require a certain amount of flair and inventiveness, baking is a science as well as an art, so unless you are very experienced, it is important to follow the recipes exactly. Read through the recipe and collect all the ingredients and equipment together before you start. Do not be tempted to cut corners. It is worth noting that there are some variables that may affect the end result, and this is where skill and experience come in. The biggest of these is usually the oven. Because oven temperatures can vary from appliance to appliance, to ensure the best results, use the baking times specified in the recipes as a guide only. Do not be tempted to check the oven too early, which could adversely affect the baked goods, but do check just a few minutes before the end of

the baking time to see how the baking is progressing. And if the food is not ready at the end of the baking time, bake for a little longer. If you are new to baking or not familiar with your oven, it is a good idea to bake a tray of fairy cakes or a Victoria Sandwich as a test run. If these cook too quickly, your oven may be operating a little hotter than the controls indicate, so either lower the oven temperature slightly or check the baked goods a little earlier than the specified time. Likewise, if the cakes take longer than expected to bake, your oven may be a little slow, so increase the temperature by a few degrees.

Most importantly, remember that baking is a fun and highly rewarding pastime, so let that knowledge encourage and inspire you to go ahead right away and prepare your own home-baked creations today.

GETTING STARTED

EQUIPMENT

Measuring scales, mixing bowls, a wooden spoon, a few baking tins and a rolling pin are all the items you need to begin baking. But as the baking bug bites, you can gradually add other tools to those basics, such as an electric whisk, which, although not essential, will certainly make the job easier and quicker.

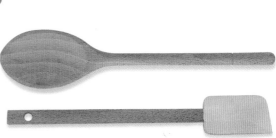

MEASURING

For successful baking, it is essential to have accurate measuring scales or cups and a set of measuring spoons. Electronic or balance scales are more accurate than measuring cups, which measure ingredients by volume. If you intend to do a lot of baking but generally use cups for measuring, it is worth investing in a set of scales to ensure success every time. It is important to bear in mind that spoon measures are always level unless otherwise stated in the recipe.

MIXING, BEATING AND BLENDING

BOWLS

You will need a selection of bowls of various sizes. Choose from ceramic, glass or stainless steel.

SPOONS

Wooden spoons come in a variety of sizes and are essential for beating ingredients together. A large metal spoon is useful for folding in flour.

SPATULAS

Plastic or silicone spatulas are ideal for scraping out bowls with the minimum of waste, as well as for folding in flour.

Flan tin

Cake tin

Springform cake tin

BAKEWARE

It is advisable to invest in a few good-quality baking tins. If looked after, they will last a lifetime, and they are less likely than inexpensive tins to twist or buckle in the oven and to cause sticking or burning. Choose ones that feel relatively heavy and do not bend easily.

The most useful to begin with are:
- Baking sheets
- 18 cm/7 inch shallow cake tins
- 20 cm/8 inch shallow cake tins
- 23 cm/9 inch shallow cake tins
- 20 cm/8 inch deep loose-bottomed or springform tin
- 20 cm/8 inch square cake tin
- 450 g/1 lb and 900 g/2 lb loaf tins
- 12 hole muffin and bun tins
- Swiss roll tin
- 20 cm/8 inch flan tin

WHISKS AND MIXERS

Electric appliances take the hard work out of creaming and whisking cake mixtures. A hand-held electric whisk is sufficient for cakes, while a free-standing mixer is useful for those who like to bake in larger quantities and for making bread. A manual balloon whisk is good for whisking egg whites and for whisked sponge mixes if you don't have or don't want to buy an electric whisk.

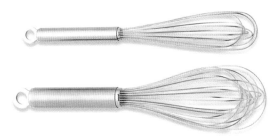

FOOD PROCESSORS

These are great for rubbing fat into flour quickly and efficiently. They can also be used to prepare cake mixtures, but tend not to incorporate as much air as mixing by hand or with a whisk, so the resulting cakes may be more dense.

INGREDIENTS

FLOUR

Wheat flour is the most commonly used flour for baking. The amount of gluten (protein) in wheat flour varies between the different types:

● **PLAIN WHITE FLOUR**
has the bran and wheat
germ removed, and is then
fortified with vitamins. Soft
plain flour is made from
wheat with a low gluten
content. It has a fine texture

and is ideal for making cakes, pastry
and biscuits. Strong plain flour is milled from wheat with a high gluten content and is used for breads and most yeast cookery.

● **SELF-RAISING FLOUR** is plain white flour with baking powder added as a raising agent. To make your own self-raising flour add 2 teaspoons of baking powder to each 225 g/8 oz plain flour.

● **WHOLEMEAL FLOUR** is flour that has
been milled from the whole of the
wheat grain. It is coarser and heavier
than white flour. It is available as a
strong (high-gluten) flour for bread
making and a soft (lower-gluten)
flour for cakes and pastry.

● Other flours such as brown flour, malted flour, cornflour and buckwheat, rye, rice and chestnut flours are also sometimes used to a limited extent in baking, each having its own unique characteristic or flavour.

SUGARS

Most sugar is produced from one of two sources: sugar cane or sugar beet. There are a number of different types of sugar, each with its own particular qualities. Unrefined sugars are made from sugar cane and have a higher mineral, vitamin and trace element content than refined sugars.

● **GRANULATED SUGAR**
can be used to achieve a
crunchy texture in some
biscuits and in cakes
prepared by the rubbing-
in method.
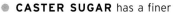

● **CASTER SUGAR** has a finer crystal and dissolves more readily. It is the type of sugar most frequently used in baking. It is known as caster sugar because it is suitable for placing in a caster - a container with a perforated top, similar to a flour dredger.

● **GOLDEN GRANULATED, GOLDEN CASTER** and **GOLDEN ICING SUGAR** are the unrefined forms of the refined sugars.

● **MOLASSES SUGAR** is a dark, fine-grained unrefined sugar with a strong flavour, used for rich fruit cakes.

● **DARK MUSCOVADO SUGAR** is an unrefined sugar that has a less intense flavour than molasses sugar, but a good, dark colour. It is ideal for light fruit cakes and gingerbread.

● **LIGHT MUSCOVADO SUGAR** is lighter in colour and flavour than the dark variety and is used widely in cakes, muffins, teabreads and biscuits.

● **DEMERARA SUGAR** is a large, coarse-grained brown sugar that can be made from either refined or unrefined sugar. As well as being used in baking, it is sometimes sprinkled over the tops of pies, crumbles and cakes for its crunchy texture.

● **SOFT LIGHT** and **DARK BROWN SUGARS** are similar to light and dark muscovado sugars. They are usually refined white sugar that has been tossed in molasses or syrup.

● **ICING SUGAR** has a very fine, powdery grain and dissolves almost instantly. It is used in some biscuits and pastry, and for making icings and fillings.

FATS

● **BUTTER** produces the best flavour. Unsalted butter is generally considered best for baking. If you do use salted butter, you will not need to add any extra salt to the recipe (except for bread making). Use butter straight from the refrigerator for pastry making and at room temperature for cake making.

● **MARGARINE** is preferred over butter by some people for baking. Block margarine is generally the best, but soft tub margarine is needed for making cakes by the all-in-one method.

● **LOW-FAT SPREADS** are not suitable for baking, as they contain a high proportion of water.

● **SUET** is used for making suet crust pastry and can be made from either shredded beef fat or solidified vegetable oils.

● **LARD** and **WHITE VEGETABLE FAT** have a bland flavour, but give a light, short texture to pastry and biscuits, so are sometimes used. They are usually combined with butter for flavour.

EGGS

The size of eggs used in baking is important. Store eggs in the refrigerator away from strong-smelling foods. Remove from the refrigerator to return to room temperature before using if possible, as cold eggs do not combine as well with other ingredients or trap as much air.

RAISING AGENTS

● **BAKING POWDER** is a mixture of cream of tartar and bicarbonate of soda. When mixed with moisture, it releases carbon dioxide, a harmless gas that expands during baking to make the food rise.

● **BICARBONATE OF SODA** produces carbon dioxide when mixed with an acid such as lemon juice or buttermilk.

● **YEAST** is a single-cell organism that converts the natural sugars in flour to produce carbon dioxide. Yeast needs warmth, moisture and food (sugars) to work. It is available in both dried and fresh forms for baking.

CAKES

Home-made cakes bring immense pleasure to both the maker and the consumer. If you are new to baking, start by making some of the family cakes and tray bakes in this book. These are some of the most basic and easy-to-prepare cakes, which are nonetheless attractive and flavoursome, and are ideal for an everyday teatime treat, for packed lunches or for a snack. Scones, teabreads and muffins also fit this bill, and children especially will love to eat these. You could ask them to choose which small cakes to bake for themselves and the rest of the family. Once you have mastered the basics, you can move on to some of the more challenging cakes and gâteaux, perfect as a centrepiece for a special occasion or as a sumptuous dessert for a dinner party.

It is essential to follow a cake recipe exactly and measure all ingredients accurately. Do not open the oven door too often, close the door gently and move tins carefully.

Always preheat the oven before you begin preparing cakes. It is important that they go into the oven at the correct temperature and very few cakes will benefit from standing around for long while waiting for the oven to heat. Also grease any baking tins before you begin.

Most cakes will freeze well for up to four months without filling or icing (although butter icing freezes well). Most will keep in an airtight container for a few days, although some baked goods are best eaten on the day they are made.

GREASING AND LINING CAKE TINS

Unless you have non-stick bakeware, you will need to grease your baking tins before using, and you may prefer to take the extra precaution of greasing non-stick tins in any case. What fat you use for greasing the tins is a matter of personal choice. A little butter or margarine can be smeared onto the tin, or use a light-flavoured oil such as sunflower, corn or vegetable oil, brushed over the entire inside surface of the tin with a pastry brush. Whichever you use, the tin just needs to be very lightly coated.

Some recipes require the baking tin to be lined. In some cases, only the base of the tin needs to be lined, which helps to ensure that the cake is successfully turned out. Use greaseproof paper or non-stick baking paper to line the tins.

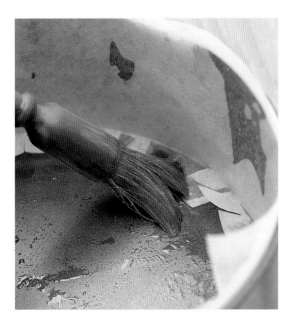

thickness strip of brown paper about 2 cm/3/4 inch deeper than the tin. Wrap around the outside of the tin and secure with string.

LINING A SHALLOW BAKING OR SWISS ROLL TIN

Cut the paper about 7.5 cm/3 inches longer and wider than the tin. Lightly grease the tin and place the paper on top. Snip at the corners and press into the tin. Lightly grease the paper.

LINING A LOAF TIN

Lightly grease the tin. Cut two strips of paper, one the width of the tin and long enough to cover the sides and base, and one the length of the tin and long enough to cover the base and sides. Press each piece into place and lightly grease.

LINING A CAKE TIN

ROUND TIN Place the tin on the paper and draw around it. Cut out the round just inside the drawn line. Cut a strip of paper about 2 cm/3/4 inch wider than the depth of the tin and long enough to go around the tin. Fold over about 1 cm/1/2 inch along one long edge and snip from the edge up to the fold at 2-cm/3/4-inch intervals along the length. Lightly grease the tin and position the strip of paper around the edge so that the snipped edge lies flat on the base of the tin. Lay the disc of paper in the base and lightly grease.

SQUARE TIN Proceed as for a round tin, folding the strip at the corners and snipping up to the fold so that the paper lies flush to the tin.

For rich fruit cakes, extra protection is needed to prevent the edges from burning or drying out during the extended cooking time. Line the tin as above, but use a double thickness of paper. Cut a double-

CAKE-MAKING METHODS

The main ingredients for making cakes are flour, fat, sugar and eggs. The proportion of fat to flour will influence the method by which the cake is made. With half or less fat to flour, the rubbing-in method is used, while with half or more fat to flour, the creaming method is used. If little or no fat is used, then whisking is the appropriate method.

CREAMED CAKES

The most well-known of cakes made by this method is the Victoria Sandwich, which uses butter, sugar, eggs and flour in equal quantities to make a light and airy cake. It makes a good base for many variations. Cakes made by this method should have a light, even texture. The higher the proportion of fat, sugar and eggs to flour, the richer the cake will be.

SPONGE FOR VICTORIA SANDWICH

175 g/6 oz unsalted butter, softened
175 g/6 oz caster sugar
3 eggs, beaten
175 g/6 oz self-raising flour

BASIC METHOD

1 Cream (beat) the butter and sugar together in a bowl until pale and fluffy. A wooden spoon or a hand-held electric whisk is ideal for this task. The more thoroughly the butter and sugar are creamed together, the lighter the texture of the cake will be. Creaming also breaks down the sugar crystals, giving a finer texture. Use sugar with small crystals such as caster or soft light brown sugar rather than the coarser granulated or demerara sugar, as these will blend with the butter more easily.

2 Gradually add the eggs, beating well after each addition. Eggs are best used at room temperature. Add any flavouring extracts or essences at this stage.

3 Sift the flour and any other fine dry ingredients. Carefully fold into the cake mixture. Use a large metal spoon or a spatula to do this and take care to incorporate the flour gently without knocking out the air you have beaten into the mixture. Use a cutting and folding-over movement.

STORAGE Cakes made by the creaming method keep well in an airtight tin. Undecorated cakes freeze well.

ALL-IN-ONE CAKES

This is a simplified variation of the creaming method. All the ingredients are beaten together at once until smooth. Extra baking powder helps to make the cake rise and soft margarine or butter is essential for it to mix fully. This gives a close-textured cake and is an ideal method when time is of the essence.

WHISKED SPONGE CAKES

These can be made with or without any fat. Whisked sponges depend on the amount of air trapped into the eggs and sugar during the whisking of the eggs. The bowl should be warmed and the eggs at room temperature. The best results are achieved by using an electric whisk. Care then has to be taken not to knock the air out when folding in the flour, which must be done with a lightness of hand.

SWISS ROLL CAKE

3 large eggs
125 g/4¹/₂ oz caster sugar
125 g/4¹/₂ oz plain flour
1 tbsp hot water

BASIC METHOD

1 Put the eggs and sugar in a warmed bowl and whisk together until very pale and thick. Air will become entangled with the albumen in the egg white and the mixture will increase considerably in volume. A good test to see if you have whisked in enough air is to try to write your initials with the mixture dropping from the whisk. If the mixture

---

CURDLING IN CAKE MIXTURE

Curdling is the term used when the water from the eggs separates out from the fat globules in the cake mixture, and is usually caused by the eggs being too cold. A curdled cake mixture will hold less air and will produce a cake with a dense texture. To help prevent curdling, use eggs at room temperature. If your mixture does begin to curdle, beat in a tablespoon of the flour to help bind the mixture back together. This is not a true curdling, which is the process of separating the curds from the whey in milk.

holds its shape long enough for you to write two initials before they disappear, the mixture is thick enough. Setting the bowl over a saucepan of hot water can help speed up the process.

2 If the mixture has been whisked over hot water, remove from the heat and continue whisking until it is cool.

3 Carefully fold in the sifted flour with a large metal spoon or spatula using a cutting and folding-over movement, blending in with a little water.

4 Drizzle over any melted butter or oil specified in the recipe and carefully fold in.

STORAGE Fat-free sponges are best eaten on the day they are made. Those with some fat will keep a little longer if stored in an airtight container.

RUBBED-IN CAKES

This method of cake mixing produces a plain, coarse texture and is most often used for teabreads, scones and buns. The proportion of fat to flour varies from 25 per cent to around 66 per cent. Rubbing in the

fat with the fingertips held high over the bowl incorporates air. Liquid is added and the mixture is then gently brought together. Be careful not to overwork the mixture or the results will be tough. Baking powder is usually added to assist the raising.

SCONE MIXTURE

225 g/8 oz self-raising flour
6 tbsp butter, cut into small pieces
15 g/$\frac{1}{2}$ oz caster sugar
pinch of salt
1 egg, beaten
50 ml/2 fl oz milk

BASIC METHOD

1 Sift the flour into a bowl.

2 Rub in the butter with your fingertips, lifting your hands high to help to incorporate air into the

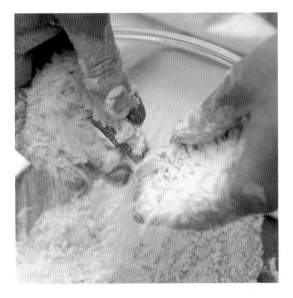

mixture. The mixture should resemble fine breadcrumbs.

3 Stir in the sugar, salt and any other dry ingredients used to flavour the cake, such as coconut or fruit.

4 Stir in the egg and milk.

STORAGE Rubbed-in cakes should be kept for no more than three days, as they tend to become dry over time.

MELTED CAKES

A few dense, moist cakes such as gingerbread employ this method. The fat and sugar are melted together before the dry ingredients are stirred in.

GINGERBREAD

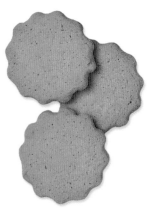

450 g/1 lb plain/all-purpose flour
1-2 tsp bicarbonate of soda
2-4 tsp ground ginger
225 g/8 oz butter
225 g/6 oz sugar (treacle
   or syrup)

BASIC METHOD

1 Sift the flour, raising agent and ground ginger into a bowl.

2 Melt the butter, sugar and/or syrup in a saucepan over a low heat until the mixture combines. Take care not to overheat.

3 Pour into the dry ingredients along with any other liquids that are used.

4 Beat to form a smooth batter consistency.

STORAGE These cakes are best if left for one day before eating to become moist. They keep well in an airtight container.

SMALL CAKES

The same basic principles and techniques for making large cakes also apply to small cakes. However, the oven temperature is usually higher and the baking time much shorter. Small cakes, each not much more than a couple of bites in size, can be cooked in a 12-hole bun tray. For more substantial individual cakes, a muffin tray can be used. Lining the tins with paper cake cases will ensure that they turn out easily. Some small cakes are made as one large cake and then cut into appropriately sized bars or squares. This is a quick way of producing individual cakes. Small cakes should be quite simply decorated or left plain.

IS IT COOKED?

Follow the timings in the recipe as a guideline, but also rely on your own judgement, as ovens vary in temperature. Small cakes should be well risen, firm and springy to the touch, and sponge cakes should also be springy to the touch.

Test by gently pressing the cake with a finger. Once you have removed your finger, the cake should spring back, but if you can still see the fingerprint, return the cake to the oven for a few minutes longer. Fruit cake and deep sponge cakes are best tested with a skewer, inserted into the centre. The skewer should come out clean when the cake is cooked.

For most cakes, leave to cool for a few minutes in the tin before turning out and transferring to a wire rack to cool completely. Some cakes such as rich fruit cakes benefit from being allowed to cool completely in the tin – the recipe will specify this where necessary.

PASTRY

Basic pastry is not as difficult to make as is sometimes perceived, and although preparing other, more specialist pastries is an area of baking that does require a certain amount of skill, by following the recipes closely, that skill can be acquired and professional results achieved with a little practice.

It is important to follow a few basic rules when making pastry. Always measure the ingredients accurately and keep everything cool. Always use a light touch and handle the pastry with care. Knead the dough just sufficiently to bind it together - over-kneading will start to develop the gluten in the flour and result in a tough, greasy pastry.

Roll out pastry lightly, taking care not to stretch it unduly. Use only a small amount of flour when rolling out to avoid upsetting the careful balance of ingredients. Allow the pastry to rest wrapped in the refrigerator before rolling.

A little salt may be added to bring out the flavour of pastry, but if salted butter or margarine is used, this is usually sufficient.

COOKING PASTRY

The oven must be hot when the pastry is first put in so that it will rise when the air that it contains is heated. The gluten in the flour absorbs the water and stretches and entangles the air in the pastry as the air expands. The heat of the oven then sets the pastry in its risen shape. As it cooks, the starch grains in the flour will also burst and absorb the fat. If the oven is too cool, the fat will melt and run out while the flour remains uncooked, resulting in a heavy, soggy and greasy pastry. After the pastry is set, the temperature can be reduced to cook the filling, if required.

TYPES OF PASTRY

All kinds of pastry, except suet crust, use plain flour. Wholemeal flour can be used instead of white, but it produces heavier results and requires extra liquid to bring it together.

SHORTCRUST PASTRY

Perhaps the most common home-baked pastry, this is also one of the easiest to master as long as the basic rules of pastry making are followed. A proportion of half fat to flour is used.

225 g/8 oz plain flour
115 g/4 oz butter
2-3 tbsp cold water

BASIC METHOD

1 Sieve the flour into a bowl.

6 Use as required, then allow the pastry to relax again in a cool place for 15-30 minutes before baking. This is especially important if you have not previously relaxed the pastry.

7 Bake in a hot oven for 15-20 minutes until set. The temperature may then be reduced.

Shortcrust pastry can be made in a food processor, which helps to keep it cooler than warm hands can. Put the flour and butter in the processor and process until the mixture resembles fine breadcrumbs. The liquid can then be added to the machine, processing until the pastry comes together. Alternatively, for greater control, tip the flour and butter mixture into a bowl and add the liquid by hand.

The proportion of fat to flour can be increased, or eggs added, to produce richer pastries such as pâté sucrée. Because of the increased fat content, these pastries can be more difficult to handle. In some cases, the fat content is so high that additional liquid is not needed to bring the pastry together. Rolling out these extra-rich pastries can be made easier by rolling the pastry between two sheets of clingfilm. Additional ingredients such as ground nuts, lemon rind, sugar or spices can be added for flavour.

2 Cut the butter into small cubes and add to the flour. Rub in using your fingertips, lifting your hand high above the bowl to incorporate more air. The mixture will resemble fine breadcrumbs when the butter has been fully rubbed in.

3 Stir in any additional flavourings, if using, such as ground nuts, cheese or sugar for sweet pastry.

4 Add the liquid all at once and use your fingers to bring the pastry together. Turn the dough out onto a lightly floured work surface and knead very lightly. Ideally, the pastry should be wrapped in foil or clingfilm and chilled in the refrigerator for 30 minutes to allow the pastry to 'relax', which helps to prevent it from shrinking when it is baked.

5 Roll out the dough on a lightly floured work surface. Rolling should be carried out in short, sharp strokes, with a light, even pressure in a forward movement only. Turn the pastry as you roll.

BAKING BLIND

When used to line a tin, shortcrust pastry is often precooked to set the pastry before the filling is added.

The term used to describe this is 'baking blind'.

1 Line the tin with the rolled-out pastry and prick the base with a fork.

2 Chill for about 30 minutes in the refrigerator or 10 minutes in the freezer (you can also bake pastry cases blind from frozen).

3 Line the pastry case with a sheet of non-stick baking paper, greaseproof paper or foil and fill with purpose-made ceramic or metal baking beans or dried pulses or rice. These baking beans help to conduct heat and cook the pastry, as well as preventing the pastry from puffing up in the centre.

4 Bake for 10 minutes, then remove the paper and beans and bake for a further 10 minutes until the pastry is just golden.

5 Remove from the oven and brush a little beaten egg or egg white over the base to seal (the heat of the pastry will cook the egg).

PUFF PASTRY

Both flaky and puff pastry are more difficult to make and very time consuming, but their richness, especially in the case of puff pastry, gives them a superior flavour. More experienced bakers will enjoy the challenge of making these pastries as well as the end results. Puff pastry has the highest proportion of fat to flour (equal proportions) and is therefore the most difficult to handle. The principle behind the pastry is to create many layers of dough and butter by folding and turning the two together. For an evenly layered pastry, it is important that you always roll it to the same thickness and that the edges are very straight and even.

350 g/12 oz plain flour

175 g/6 oz butter

8 tbsp cold water

BASIC METHOD

1 Sift the flour into a bowl and rub in one-quarter of the butter.

2 Add the water and use your fingers to bring the pastry together. Knead briefly to form a smooth dough. Put in a polythene bag and chill in the refrigerator for 30 minutes.

3 Roll out the remaining butter between 2 sheets of clingfilm to form a block about 1 cm/^{1}/2 inch thick.

4 Roll out the dough to a square about 4 times the size of the block of butter.

5 Put the block of butter in the centre of the dough and fold over the corners of the dough to completely enclose the butter.

6 Roll out the dough into a rectangle 3 times as long as it is wide.

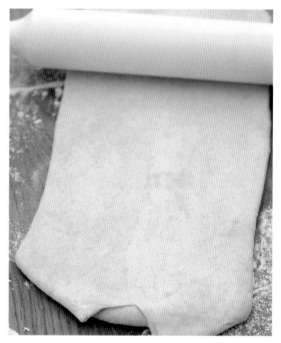

7 Fold one-third of the dough over to cover the middle third, then fold the remainder over the top.

8 Give the dough a half turn, roll out to form another rectangle and fold again as before. Repeat the initial rolling and folding 6 times in total, chilling the dough frequently between rolling.

9 Leave to relax for a final 30 minutes, then use as required. Trim the folded edges of the pastry before using to assist the rising. Bake in a hot oven. The pastry should rise 6-8 times its original height.

FLAKY PASTRY

This uses a slightly lower proportion of fat to flour – two-thirds to three-quarters fat to flour – and the fat is added in stages. It is advisable to use a strong plain flour for flaky pastry. After the initial fat has been added, the dough is kneaded to develop the elasticity of the gluten, resulting in an elastic dough that will rise easily. A little lemon juice can be added to help develop the gluten and counteract the richness of the pastry. The pastry must be allowed to relax before being baked. Once cooked, the pastry does not keep long unless frozen, although the uncooked pastry can be stored in the refrigerator for up to 48 hours. Uncooked pastry can also be sealed and frozen for up to four months.

225 g/8 oz plain flour
175 g/6 oz butter
6-7 tbsp cold milk or water

BASIC METHOD

1 Sift the flour into a bowl and rub in one-quarter of the butter.

2 Add the water and use your fingers to bring the pastry together. Knead briefly to form a smooth dough.

3 Roll out the dough into a rectangle 3 times as long as it is wide.

4 Dot one-third of the remaining butter over two-thirds of the pastry in rough lumps. Fold the uncovered dough over to cover half the buttered dough, then fold the remaining third over the top.

5 Seal the edges of the dough by pressing down with a rolling pin.

6 Give the dough a half turn, roll out to form another rectangle and repeat steps 4 and 5 twice more until all the butter has been used. Put the pastry in a polythene bag and chill in the refrigerator for 30 minutes.

7 Roll and fold the pastry 3 more times as before, but without the addition of butter. Leave to relax for a final 30 minutes, then use as required. Trim the folded edges of the pastry before using to assist the rising. Bake in a hot oven.

ROUGH PUFF

This pastry is relatively easy to make and produces a fabulous light, flaky pastry. It can be a little sticky to handle to begin with. It has a similar fat content to flaky pastry.

225 g/8 oz plain flour
175 g/6 oz butter
6–7 tbsp cold milk or water

BASIC METHOD

1 Sift the flour into a bowl. Cut the butter into lumps a little smaller than the size of a walnut and add to the flour.

2 Add the water and use your fingers to bring the pastry together. Knead very lightly.

3 Roll and fold the pastry as for puff pastry.

4 Chill for 30 minutes before using and bake in a hot oven.

SUET CRUST PASTRY

Suet crust pastry is a filling, homely kind of pastry. Self-raising flour or plain flour and baking powder is used to make this.

225 g/8 oz plain flour
115 g/4 oz suet
2 tsp baking powder
150 ml/5 fl oz cold water

BASIC METHOD

1 Sift the flour into a bowl.

2 Stir in the suet and baking powder.

3 Add enough water to form an elastic dough.

4 Only roll out the dough once to prevent producing a hard pastry.

COVERING A PIE

This is the basic method for making a single crust to cover a savoury or sweet pie filling. You can then add decorative details and a glaze to enhance the appearance of the pie.

1 Roll out the pastry to about 5 cm/ 2 inches larger all round than the top of the dish.

2 Cut a strip about 2.5 cm/1 inch wide from the edge of the pastry.

3 Moisten the edge of the dish and stick the pastry strip to the dish.

4 Fill the pie and dampen the pastry strip with a little water.

5 Using a rolling pin, carefully lift the pastry over the pie. Press the edge down to seal.

6 Using a sharp knife, trim the edge and make a small hole in the centre of the pie to allow the steam to escape.

HOT WATERCRUST PASTRY

This traditional type of pastry is used for raised pies, such as pork or game pies. It is the exception to one of the basic rules of pastry making in that its success depends on the warmth of the utensils and flour throughout the making and shaping. If it becomes too cold, it will be difficult to handle.

225 g/8 oz plain flour
85 g/3 oz lard
5 tbsp water

BASIC METHOD

1 Sift the flour into a bowl and make a well in the centre.

2 Put the lard and water in a saucepan and heat until the lard melts, then bring to the boil. Immediately add to the well in the flour and mix with a spoon to form a dough, then knead the dough.

3 The pastry should be shaped while still warm and cooked in a hot oven.

CHOUX PASTRY

This is a rich, soft pastry that relies predominately on its high water content, which becomes very hot during cooking to form a hollow pastry shell.

85 g/3 oz strong plain flour
55 g/2 oz butter
150 ml/5 fl oz water
2 eggs

BASIC METHOD

1 Sift the flour.

2 Put the butter and water in a saucepan and heat until the butter melts.

3 Add the flour to the saucepan all at once and beat with a wooden spoon until the mixture forms a ball around the spoon. Leave to cool slightly.

4 Gradually beat in the eggs until the dough is smooth and glossy. The more the mixture is beaten, the better the results, as the more air is incorporated.

5 Shape by piping or spoon, as required. Bake in a hot oven.

PASTRY FINISHES

● Use a blunt knife to tap the edge of the pie and knock it up. This also helps to seal the pie fully.

● Press the edge with a floured fork.

● Press one thumb around the edge while you pinch the outside edge between your other thumb and forefinger.

● Press a thumb around the edge and draw a knife in a short distance from the edge towards the centre of the pie between each thumbprint to create a scalloped edge.

● Decorate the pie by using the pastry trimmings. Cut them into leaves or other shapes, as desired, and stick to the pastry crust by moistening slightly.

GLAZES

Glazing the pastry will produce a shiny golden surface once baked. You can use milk, beaten egg mixed with a little water, or lightly beaten egg white for glazing. Brush a thin layer over the pastry with a pastry brush, but avoid making the pastry too wet. For sweet pies, a little caster sugar can also be sprinkled on top.

BISCUITS

Biscuit or cookie – the choice of name is yours. Americans use the latter term, while the British use the word 'biscuit' like the French, which means 'twice baked'. However, in recent times the name 'cookie' has been widely adopted along with the spread in popularity of the traditionally American-style chunky variety, such as the chocolate chip cookie. But whatever you call them and whether they are melt-in-the-mouth crumbly or deliciously chewy, home-made biscuits are always a real treat. The range and variety is almost endless – spicy, fruity, nutty, wafer-thin or thick bars, to mention but a few kinds. You can find a biscuit that is perfect for any occasion, be it a decadent coffee morning, hearty afternoon tea, an elegant dinner or a packed lunch on the run.

Because biscuits cook quickly, you will need to keep a close eye on the baking until you become more experienced in gauging the exact cooking time easily. For most biscuits, leave to cool on the baking sheet for a few minutes before transferring to a wire rack to cool completely. Many biscuits are very soft when they come out of the oven but crisp on cooling, so remember to remove them from the tin before they become completely cold or they may stick.

Store in an airtight container to retain freshness and crispness. Most biscuits also freeze well – simply thaw at room temperature.

ROLLED AND MOULDED BISCUITS

Here the biscuit dough is rolled out and cut out or shaped into logs, balls or crescents. Take care not to add too much extra flour when rolling and shaping, as this will alter the careful balance of the ingredients. If a dough is very soft, you may find it easier to roll out between two sheets of clingfilm. Try to avoid re-rolling too many times, or the biscuits may become tough.

DROP BISCUITS

These are the quickest and easiest to make. They are often made by the creaming method, where the fat and sugar are beaten together, then the flour and any additional flavourings such as nuts or chocolate chips are added. The mixture is then beaten just enough to bring all the ingredients together in a soft dough, which can then be dropped onto the baking sheet from spoons. Always place well spaced apart on the baking sheet, as the biscuits will spread during baking.

PIPED BISCUITS

Some biscuits are piped from a plain or fluted piping nozzle to produce a decorative effect. The consistency of the biscuit dough needs to be just right – too stiff and the dough will be hard to pipe; too soft and the biscuits will lose their shape when baked.

WAFERS

Some classic biscuits are very thin and crisp. The mixture is very soft (that of a batter) and is spooned onto a baking sheet and spread out to form a round. These are probably the hardest biscuits to bake, as they bake very rapidly. They are sometimes shaped into rolls or curled. In this case, you need to work fast, only baking a couple at a time, as they need to be shaped while still warm.

SLICED BISCUITS

The dough in this instance is firm and can be shaped into a log. The individual biscuits are then sliced at the desired thickness. The uncooked biscuit dough can be stored in the refrigerator for several days and a few biscuits cut and baked from the log as desired. This is an ideal way of making freshly baked biscuits every day.

BREADS AND YEAST COOKERY

There are so many different kinds of home-made bread that they can easily fill a book in themselves. Many, like soda bread, plain white bread, malt bread and rolls are great basics, but once mastered, the temptation to move on to making delicious flavoured breads is hard to resist. Not all breads rely on yeast as a raising agent and you will find a selection of breads made without yeast in this book. Sweet yeast breads and buns are delicious for high tea, breakfast or a snack.

Yeast cookery is not particularly difficult and the results are most rewarding. Unlike when working with pastry, a warm kitchen will help you on the way. Also, there is no need for the caution in handling that pastry requires - a firm hand is perfect for kneading the dough to develop the gluten content of the bread, which gives it its unique texture. Of course, you do need to allow more time to produce yeasted products, but for the most part they can be left alone to rise and prove while you are free to do other things.

Most yeasted breads and bakes freeze well, so when time is plentiful, they are ideal for batch baking. The frozen bakes can be thawed at room temperature and refreshed in a hot oven for 5 minutes to warm through before serving.

TYPES OF YEAST

Yeast is the raising agent most frequently used for breads. It is a living organism that, when active, creates carbon dioxide. Small bubbles of carbon dioxide then become trapped within the structure of the dough, giving bread its characteristic structure.

There are two main types of bread yeasts available: fresh and dried.

FRESH YEAST

This can be purchased from health food shops and some bakeries. It has a creamy colour and is moist and firm. Fresh yeast is usually dissolved in the liquid and allowed a preliminary fermentation before adding to the remaining ingredients. It will only keep for a few days in the refrigerator, but can be frozen for up to three months.

GLUTEN

Gluten is formed by a combination of two proteins, gliadin and glutenin, which are found in wheat flour. Strong flours have a higher proportion of these proteins than soft flour. When these proteins are hydrated, they bond with each other, creating a large protein called gluten that gives the bread its structure. The longer the dough is kneaded, the stronger the gluten becomes and the better texture the bread has. It is possible to knead the dough so much that it becomes too warm and the gluten begins to break down, but this is very unlikely to happen if kneading by hand. If you choose to knead in a mixer, knead for short bursts, allowing a few seconds each time for the dough to cool slightly.

DRIED YEAST

This is available in two forms. Regular dried yeast requires a preliminary fermentation and is activated by mixing with a little liquid and sugar or flour. Easy-blend dried yeast, fast-action dried yeast and instant dried yeast are all the same, but just different names for yeast that does not require this preliminary fermentation and is simply stirred into the flour before the liquid is added. The first rising and knocking back can also be eliminated if time is short. Dried yeast has a longer shelf life than fresh yeast and does not need to be refrigerated.

EFFECTS OF TEMPERATURE ON YEAST

Yeast works quickest in warm temperatures, so it is generally recommended that the dough is left in a warm place to rise. However, yeast does not stop working at lower temperatures – it simply slows down. Therefore, dough can be made, shaped and then left to rise overnight in a refrigerator. Allow the dough to return to room temperature before baking. Yeast that is left to work in slower conditions produces a loaf that many people regard as having more flavour and character.

EFFECTS OF OTHER INGREDIENTS ON YEAST ACTION

A basic loaf consists of just flour, yeast, salt and water, but some breads as well as buns, cakes and even pastries are made with yeast doughs that have been enriched with other ingredients such as butter, sugar and eggs. Additional ingredients may contribute to the rising, give added colour to the crumb and crust and may also improve the keeping qualities. However, all these additional ingredients will have an effect on the action of yeast.

● Sugar in small amounts speeds up the action of yeast, but in larger quantities – above 55 g/2 oz per 450 g/1 lb – it will retard the action of yeast.

● Fat in proportions above 25 g/1 oz per 450 g/1 lb will retard the action of yeast.

● Eggs, because of their fat content, may slow the action of yeast, but they also have the ability to retain air in the mixture, so often help to produce a lighter texture.

To overcome any adverse effects of these added ingredients:

● Allow additional time for the rising – 2 hours or more is not unusual.

● Make the dough in two parts, with the additional ingredients added after an initial rising.

● Extra yeast may be added.

A NOTE ABOUT SALT

Salt is an essential ingredient in bread making, as it not only adds flavour but also strengthens the gluten structure, and helps control the growth of yeast. Too little and the result will be a poor gluten structure; too much and the salt will inhibit the action of the yeast. Both will result in a loaf of poor volume and flavour. For this reason, it is important not to vary the amount of salt in a recipe, even if you are trying to reduce your salt intake, as this will adversely affect the finished product.

MAKING YEAST BREADS

BASIC METHOD

The method used is basically the same for all yeast breads, although individual steps may vary according to the recipe.

675 g/1^1/$_2$ lb strong plain bread flour
2 tsp salt
2 tsp easy blend yeast
about 450 ml/^{3}/$_4$ pt luke warm water
2 tbsp olive oil or 25 g/1 oz butter

1 Sift the flour and salt into a large bowl. Stir in the easy-blend dried yeast, and make a well in the centre. Pour in the liquid and mix to a soft, sticky dough.

2 Turn out the dough onto a lightly floured work surface and begin kneading by folding the dough over on top of itself and pushing away with the heel of your hand – do not be afraid to be quite forceful. Keep kneading, giving the dough a quarter turn as you do so, for 10 minutes, or until the dough is very smooth and elastic and no longer sticky. Alternatively, knead the dough in an electric mixer fitted with a dough hook for 6-8 minutes.

3 Form the dough into a ball and put in a lightly oiled bowl. Rub a little oil over the surface of the dough to prevent it drying out and cover loosely with clingfilm or slide the bowl inside a clean plastic carrier bag. Leave to rise in a warm place for 1 hour, or until doubled in size.

4 When the dough has increased to double its original size, turn out onto a lightly floured work surface and lightly knead again for a few minutes. This is called 'knocking back', as some of the air that has been incorporated into the dough is knocked out and the dough shrinks in size. This ensures that the bread has a more even texture, as any large air pockets are removed at this stage.

5 Shape the dough as required and place in a lightly greased baking tin or tray. If placing in a tin, the dough should half-fill the tin.

6 Cover loosely again and leave to rise (prove) for a second time until doubled in size.

7 Bake in a hot oven. To test if the bread is cooked, turn out of the tin and tap the base. The loaf should sound hollow. Leave to cool on a wire rack.

YEAST-FREE BREADS

Some breads do not contain yeast. These breads use another method to leaven the bread (make the bread rise) or are unleavened. Sometimes called quick breads, soda bread and corn bread fall into the former category. Bicarbonate of soda or baking powder is added to the dough. These produce carbon dioxide, a process that begins as soon as the dough is mixed, so the bread must be baked immediately. The dough should be soft and sticky, and in some cases is more like a thick batter. Quick breads have a soft, crumbly texture and some are best served warm. Most are best eaten the day they are made.

Unleavened breads are sometimes called flat breads. Some flat breads, such as naan and pitta bread are in fact leavened with yeast or baking powder but unleavened dough can also be used. Flat breads are among the oldest breads. Evidence has been found that they were cooked on stones in Neolithic times. Paratha, tortillas and chapattis are all examples of yeast-free flat breads. In the modern home, they can be cooked on a griddle or in a heavy-based frying pan. Flat breads can be topped like pizza and focaccia, stuffed like pita bread, filled with beans and rice and rolled like chapattis or tortillas, or used for dipping like poppadums from India.

BREAD MACHINES

You can make bread with the minimum of fuss and effort by using a bread machine. Once all the ingredients have been weighed and added to the pan, the machine can be left to do the hard work and a few hours later you have a freshly baked loaf. Although some of the fun of making bread is removed, it is nevertheless a very convenient way of producing freshly baked, warm bread, and as most machines have a timer, you can set it so that you can enjoy it when you wake up in the morning. Always follow the manufacturer's instructions, as quantities of ingredients and methods may vary.

WHAT WENT WRONG?

Accurate measuring and careful following of the recipe should ensure success. However, when things do go wrong, there is often a simple reason, and if you identify the cause, the mistake can be avoided in the future. Baking does not have to be absolutely perfect every time. Little imperfections and variations add to the charm of home baking and distinguish the end results from the rather dull, characterless mass-produced baked goods.

CAKES

SUNK IN THE MIDDLE
- Cake slightly undercooked
- Oven door being opened too early
- Mixture too wet
- Over-beating of the fat and sugar
- Too much raising agent
- Oven temperature too low

UNEVEN RISE
- Mixture not spread in tin evenly
- Flour not folded in evenly (whisked sponges)
- Oven not properly preheated
- Oven or oven shelves not level

PEAKED OR CRACKED TOP
- Baking in too hot an oven so that the crust cooks too quickly – as the cake's centre cooks and rises, it is forced to push through the cooked crust, causing it to crack
- Too much mixture in the tin
- Too much raising agent
- Mixture too wet or too dry
- Cooking too near the top of the oven (again cooking the crust too quickly)

CRUST TOO PALE
- Cake cooked too low in the oven
- Oven overloaded
- Oven too cool

CRUST TOO DARK
- Cake cooked too near the top of the oven
- Oven temperature too high
- Tin too large
- Baked too long
- Cake not protected with paper (rich fruit cake)

SPECKLED TOP
- Insufficient beating of fat and sugar
- Granulated or demerara sugar used

CRACKED SWISS ROLL
- Mixture too dry
- Too much mixture in tin
- Overcooked
- Rolled up when cold

SUNKEN FRUIT
- Mixture too wet to support the fruit
- Fruit too large and heavy
- Wet fruit; tossing in a little flour may help
- Oven temperature too low
- Opening door during cooking

SHORTCRUST PASTRY

DIFFICULT TO ROLL
- Too dry

- Self-raising flour used instead of plain flour
- Too much fat
- Overmixed

EXCESSIVE SHRINKING

- Over-handling
- Pastry stretched when rolling
- Not allowing pastry to rest before baking

SOGGY PASTRY

- Not fully cooked
- Too much liquid
- Pie cover placed over hot filling
- No vent for steam to escape (pies)
- Filling poured into pastry case that has cracks or holes in (tarts and flans) - seal with a little beaten egg after baking blind

HARD OR TOUGH PASTRY

- Overhandling
- Too little fat
- Too much liquid
- Oven temperature too low

TARTS WITH RISEN CENTRE OR COLLAPSED SIDES

- Self-raising flour used instead of plain flour
- Pastry not pricked before baking
- Not weighted with baking beans during blind baking

BLISTERED CRUST

- Water not evenly mixed in
- Fat not properly rubbed in

CHOUX PASTRY
PASTE TOO THIN

- Water not boiled when flour added
- Inaccurate number of eggs

PASTE TOO THICK

- Liquid boiled for too long
- Wrong egg size

CLOSE, HEAVY TEXTURE

- Insufficient beating
- Oven temperature too low

BADLY CRACKED

- Oven temperature too high

BREAD
INSUFFICIENT RISING

- Too little yeast
- Too little sugar
- Too much salt
- Yeast out of date
- Insufficient time proving (for rich yeast mixture)
- Proving at too low a temperature

BREAD RISEN TOO MUCH

- Too much yeast
- Too little salt

SUNK IN THE CENTRE

- Too much liquid
- Too little salt
- Too much yeast
- Over-proving

CENTRE SOGGY

- Too much of the wet ingredients/water
- Oven temperature too high

DAMP CRUST

- Left in the tin too long after baking
- Wrapped while warm

CRUST TOO DARK

- Too much sugar
- Cooked too long or at too high a temperature

DENSE TEXTURE

- Not enough liquid
- Soft flour used
- Insufficient kneading
- Too much salt
- Liquid too hot (kills the yeast)
- Grains without sufficient gluten used

COARSE, OPEN TEXTURE

- Too much liquid
- Overproving
- Oven temperature too low

FLAT TOP

- Flour too soft
- Dough too wet

GLOSSARY OF BAKING TERMS

BAIN-MARIE

This is a water bath. The baking tin or dish is placed in another containing hot water, resulting in very gentle cooking.

BAKE BLIND

The term given to the process of par-baking pastry cases.

BAKING BEANS

Used to weight pastry down while baking blind. Baking beans can be purpose-made ceramic or metal beans, or dried pulses or rice. All can be reused again and again for this purpose.

BEAT

Method of incorporating air into ingredients, or combining or softening an ingredient with a spoon, whisk or fork.

CREAMING

The process of beating sugar and fat together until the mixture is creamy in both colour and texture.

DOUGH

A mixture of flour and liquids, dough can be described as either soft or firm, depending on its stiffness.

DREDGE

Sprinkle generously.

DUST

Sprinkle lightly.

FERMENTATION

A term used to describe the chemical action produced by yeast as it converts sugars in the flour to carbon dioxide and alcohol (which evaporates during baking).

FOLDING IN

The term used to describe carefully incorporating flour into a mixture using a cutting and folding-over movement.

GLAZE

A thin, shiny coating that may be of egg, egg white, milk, water, jam or jelly.

GLUTEN

Proteins in flour that can be developed by kneading in the form of a dough and making the dough elastic.

KNEAD

Working together of a dough with the hands. For pastry, scones and biscuits, light kneading is required. For bread, heavy, prolonged kneading is required to develop the gluten.

KNOCK BACK

To knead dough for a second time after the first rising. This helps to ensure an even texture.

PIPING

The process of pushing a mixture through a bag fitted with a piping nozzle to shape. Some biscuits and choux pastry can be piped to shape. Piping is also used to shape icing to decorate cakes or biscuits.

PROVE

To leave bread to rise a second time after knocking back and shaping it.

RUB IN

Rub fat into flour with the fingertips until evenly distributed.

SIFT

To shake dry ingredients through a sieve. Sifting flour helps to incorporate air.

SYRUP

A concentrated solution of sugar in water.

UNLEAVENED

A term used for breads that do not use a raising agent.

WHIP

The same as whisk, but is usually used in relation to cream and creamy mixtures.

WHISK

To beat ingredients rapidly to incorporate air into them.

biscuits

There's a biscuit for every occasion. Equally at home on a fine china plate as packed into a plastic lunchbox, the beauty of biscuits is that they can be dressed up or down simply depending on their shape, decoration and ingredients. Whether melt-in-the-mouth soft or deliciously chewy, the different varieties are endless. Choose from spicy, nutty, thin or thick bars, not to mention the many different shapes found in this chapter. As well as the regular 'cut' biscuits there are sliced biscuits, piped biscuits, moulded biscuits, shaped biscuits, dropped biscuits and wafer biscuits. But whatever type of biscuit you go for, do not forget to check them as they bake to avoid overcooking!

MELTING HEARTS

MAKES 24

140 g/5 oz plain flour, plus extra
    for dusting

1¹/2 tsp ground mixed spice

¹/2 tsp ground ginger

pinch of salt

¹/2 tsp bicarbonate of soda

115 g/4 oz butter or margarine, plus
    extra for greasing

100 g/3¹/2 oz soft light brown sugar

2 small eggs

1 tsp cocoa powder

¹/2 tsp Kahlúa

125 ml/4 fl oz double cream or
    soured cream

12 fresh mint sprigs, to decorate

35 g/1¹/4 oz hazelnuts, toasted and
    roughly chopped, to serve

Sift the flour, mixed spice, ginger, salt and bicarbonate of soda together into a large bowl. Cream the butter and sugar together in a separate bowl until pale and fluffy, then beat in the eggs. Gradually add the cocoa powder, Kahlúa and flour mixture and continue beating until smooth. Cover with clingfilm and chill in the refrigerator for at least 8 hours or overnight if possible.

When ready to bake, preheat the oven to 180°C/350°F/Gas Mark 4 and grease a baking sheet. Roll out the dough on a lightly floured work surface into a rectangle about 3 mm/¹/8 inch thick, then cut out 24 heart shapes using a biscuit cutter or a sharp knife. Transfer to the prepared baking sheet. Bake in the preheated oven for 15 minutes, or until golden brown.

Transfer to a wire rack. When cool, serve with double cream or soured cream topped with mint sprigs. Sprinkle over the hazelnuts.

Serve these little heart-shaped biscuits with a cup of coffee, or to round off a romantic Valentine's Day dinner.

HAZELNUT BITES

Preheat the oven to 180°C/350°F/Gas Mark 4. Grease a large baking sheet or sheets. Cream the butter and sugar together in a bowl until pale and fluffy. Add the egg and almond extract and beat well. Sift the flour, baking powder and salt together into a separate bowl, then beat in the creamed mixture. Stir in the oats, chocolate chips and half the nuts.

Drop 24 teaspoonfuls of the dough onto the prepared baking sheet or sheets and flatten with a rolling pin. Bake in the preheated oven for 10 minutes, or until golden brown.

Transfer to a wire rack and leave to cool completely. Melt the chocolate pieces in a heatproof bowl set over a saucepan of barely simmering water. Cover the tops of the biscuits with the melted chocolate, then top with a sprinkling of the remaining hazelnuts. Leave to set on greaseproof paper before serving. Store the biscuits in an airtight container in the refrigerator.

MAKES 24

115 g/4 oz butter, plus extra
    for greasing
140 g/5 oz demerara sugar
1 egg
1 tbsp almond extract
140 g/5 oz plain flour
3/4 tsp baking powder
pinch of salt
175 g/6 oz rolled oats
85 g/3 oz plain chocolate chips
100 g/3½ oz hazelnuts, toasted
    and chopped
300 g/10½ oz plain chocolate pieces

Toasted hazelnuts and chocolate
partner each other very successfully.
Use milk or white chocolate
if preferred.

CANDIED FRUIT BISCUITS

A flavourful addition to the biscuit tin, these biscuits are delicious at any time of the day. Store for up to a week.

MAKES 20

2 egg whites

225 g/8 oz blanched almonds, finely ground

140 g/5 oz caster sugar

1 tsp finely grated orange rind

¹/₂ tsp ground cinnamon

2 tbsp candied fruit, plus extra to decorate

demerara sugar, for sprinkling

Preheat the oven to 180°C/350°F/Gas Mark 4. Line 2 large baking sheets with non-stick baking paper.

Beat the egg whites in a large bowl until stiff. Using a knife, gently fold in the ground almonds, caster sugar, orange rind, cinnamon and fruit until smooth.

Transfer the mixture to a piping bag fitted with a large nozzle (at least 1 cm/¹/₂ inch in diameter). Pipe 20 x 7.5-cm/3-inch rounds onto the baking paper, spaced well apart to allow for spreading. Sprinkle with the demerara sugar.

Bake in the preheated oven for 20 minutes, or until light brown.

Transfer to a wire rack. Decorate with candied fruit and leave to cool completely before serving.

COFFEE WHOLEMEAL BAKES

Preheat the oven to 190°C/375°F/Gas Mark 5. Grease a large baking sheet. Cream the butter and sugar together in a bowl until pale and fluffy. Add the egg and beat well.

Sift the white flour, bicarbonate of soda and salt together into a separate bowl, then stir in the wholemeal flour and bran. Beat in the creamed mixture, then stir in the chocolate chips, oats, coffee and hazelnuts. Mix well, using an electric mixer if preferred.

Drop 24 rounded tablespoonfuls of the mixture onto the prepared baking sheet, spaced well apart to allow for spreading.

Alternatively, with lightly floured hands, break off pieces of the mixture and roll into balls (about 25 g/1 oz each), put on the baking sheet and flatten with the back of a teaspoon.

Bake the biscuits in the preheated oven for 16–18 minutes, or until golden brown.

Transfer to a wire rack and leave to cool before serving.

MAKES 24

175 g/6 oz butter or margarine, plus extra for greasing

200 g/7 oz soft light brown sugar

1 egg

70 g/2$^{1}/_{2}$ oz plain white flour, plus extra for dusting

1 tsp bicarbonate of soda

pinch of salt

70 g/2$^{1}/_{2}$ oz plain wholemeal flour

1 tbsp bran

225 g/8 oz plain chocolate chips

185 g/6$^{1}/_{2}$ oz rolled oats

1 tbsp cold strong black coffee

100 g/3$^{1}/_{2}$ oz hazelnuts, toasted and roughly chopped

These delicious, dark biscuits, flavoured with coffee and toasted chopped hazelnuts, are perfect served with coffee.

GINGERBREAD PEOPLE

Preheat the oven to 160°C/ 325°F/Gas Mark 3. Grease 3 large baking sheets. Sift the flour, ginger, mixed spice and bicarbonate of soda together into a large bowl. Put the butter, syrup and muscovado sugar in a saucepan over a low heat and stir until melted. Pour onto the flour mixture and add the egg. Mix together to make a dough. The dough will be sticky to start with, but will become firmer as it cools.

Roll out the dough on a lightly floured work surface to about 3 mm/ ^{1}/8 inch thick, then cut out about 20 gingerbread people using a biscuit cutter. Transfer to the prepared baking sheets. Decorate with currants for eyes and pieces of cherry for mouths.

Bake the biscuits in the preheated oven for 15-20 minutes, or until firm and lightly browned.

Leave to cool on the baking sheets for a few minutes, then transfer to wire racks and leave to cool completely. Mix the icing sugar with the water in a small bowl to a thick consistency. Transfer the icing to a small polythene bag and cut a tiny hole in one corner. Use to pipe buttons or bows onto the biscuits.

MAKES 20

450 g/1 lb plain flour, plus extra
   for dusting

2 tsp ground ginger

1 tsp ground mixed spice

2 tsp bicarbonate of soda

115 g/4 oz butter, plus extra
   for greasing

100 g/3^1/2 oz golden syrup

115 g/4 oz light muscovado sugar

1 egg, beaten

TO DECORATE

currants

glacé cherries

85 g/3 oz icing sugar

3-4 tsp water

This is a favourite with children, who love to make the gingerbread shapes.
The recipe makes a pliable dough that is very easy to handle.

At Christmas, cut out star and bell shapes. When the biscuits come out of the oven,
gently pierce a hole in each one with a skewer. Thread ribbons through and
hang on the Christmas tree.

53

OATY PECAN BISCUITS

Preheat the oven to 180°C/350°F/Gas Mark 4. Grease 2 baking sheets. Cream the butter and sugar together in a bowl until pale and fluffy. Gradually beat in the egg, then stir in the nuts.

Sift the flour and baking powder together into the creamed mixture and add the oats. Stir together until well combined. Drop 15 dessertspoonfuls of the mixture onto the prepared baking sheets, spaced well apart to allow for spreading.

Bake in the preheated oven for 15 minutes, or until pale golden. Leave to cool on the baking sheets for 2 minutes, then transfer to wire racks and leave to cool completely.

MAKES 15

115 g/4 oz butter, softened, plus extra for greasing

85 g/3 oz light muscovado sugar

1 egg, beaten

55 g/2 oz pecan nuts, chopped

85 g/3 oz plain flour

1/2 tsp baking powder

55 g/2 oz rolled oats

These light, crisp biscuits are delicious just as they are, but they also taste exceptionally good served with cheese.

For a slightly different taste, substitute other chopped nuts for the pecan nuts, such as walnuts or hazelnuts.

To save a lot of hard work, cream the butter and sugar together with a hand-held electric whisk. Alternatively, use a food processor.

ORANGE HORNS

It is much easier to shape these biscuits into horn shapes while they are still warm from the oven. Leave them to cool before serving.

MAKES 30

115 g/4 oz butter or margarine, plus
    extra for greasing
125 g/4^1/2 oz soft light brown sugar
pinch of salt
1 egg white, lightly beaten
^{1}/2 tsp baking powder
85 g/3 oz oatmeal
150 g/5^1/2 oz finely chopped Brazil
    nuts or hazelnuts
1 tbsp milk
grated rind of 1 orange
1 tsp orange juice

Preheat the oven to 160ºC/325ºF/Gas Mark 3. Lightly grease a large baking sheet.

Cream the butter and sugar together in a bowl until pale and fluffy. Add the remaining ingredients and mix thoroughly.

Drop 30 rounded teaspoonfuls of the mixture onto the prepared baking sheet and flatten into small rounds using the bottom of a glass.

Bake in the preheated oven for 7 minutes.

Leave to cool slightly, then lay each biscuit in turn on a rolling pin to help start the desired curve, completing the horn shape by hand, while the biscuit is still warm.

Transfer to a wire rack and leave to cool completely before serving.

PEANUT BUTTER BISCUITS

Beat the butter and peanut butter together in a large bowl. Gradually add the sugar and beat well.

Add the egg, a little at a time, beating well after each addition, until thoroughly combined.

Sift the flour, baking powder and salt together into the mixture. Add the peanuts and mix together to form a soft dough. Wrap in clingfilm and chill in the refrigerator for 30 minutes.

When ready to bake, preheat the oven to 180°C/350°F/Gas Mark 4. Lightly grease 2 baking sheets.

Roll the dough into 20 balls on a lightly floured work surface. Transfer to the prepared baking sheets, spaced about 5 cm/2 inches apart to allow for spreading. Flatten slightly with your hand.

Bake in the preheated oven for 15 minutes, or until golden brown.

Transfer to a wire rack and leave to cool before serving.

MAKES 20

115 g/4 oz butter, softened, plus extra
   for greasing

115 g/4 oz crunchy peanut butter

225 g/8 oz granulated sugar

1 egg, lightly beaten

150 g/5$\frac{1}{2}$ oz plain flour, plus extra
   for dusting

$\frac{1}{2}$ tsp baking powder

pinch of salt

75 g/2$\frac{3}{4}$ oz chopped unsalted
   peanuts

For extra crunch and a sparkling appearance, sprinkle the biscuits with demerara sugar before baking.

LEMON JUMBLES

Preheat the oven to 160°C/325°F/Gas Mark 3. Lightly grease several baking sheets.

Cream the butter, caster sugar and lemon rind together in a bowl until pale and fluffy.

Add the beaten egg and lemon juice, a little at a time, beating well after each addition, until thoroughly combined.

Sift the flour and baking powder together into the mixture and mix together. Add the milk and mix to form a firm dough.

Turn out the dough onto a lightly floured work surface and divide into about 50 equal pieces.

Roll each piece into a sausage shape with your hands and twist in the middle to make an 'S' shape. Transfer to the prepared baking sheets.

Bake in the preheated oven for 15-20 minutes. Transfer to wire racks and leave to cool completely. Dredge the biscuits generously with icing sugar before serving.

MAKES ABOUT 50

75 g/2³/4 oz butter, softened, plus
    extra for greasing

115 g/4 oz caster sugar

grated rind of 1 lemon

1 egg, lightly beaten

4 tbsp lemon juice

350 g/12 oz plain flour, plus extra
    for dusting

1 tsp baking powder

1 tbsp milk

icing sugar, for dredging

If you prefer, shape the dough into other shapes – letters of the alphabet or geometric shapes – or just form into round biscuits.

59

SUGARED ORANGE DIAMONDS

Wrapped in cellophane and tied with ribbon, these Cointreau-flavoured biscuits would make an attractive gift.

MAKES 24

115 g/4 oz butter or margarine, plus
   extra for greasing

140 g/5 oz demerara sugar

2 tbsp orange juice

1 tbsp Cointreau

350 g/12 oz plain flour, sifted, plus
   extra for dusting

175 g/6 oz walnuts, roughly chopped

1 tbsp finely grated orange rind

icing sugar, for dusting

Beat the butter, demerara sugar, orange juice and Cointreau together in a bowl until pale and fluffy.

Mix the flour, walnuts and orange rind together in a separate bowl. Add the creamed mixture and mix until thoroughly combined. Cover with clingfilm and chill in the refrigerator for 2 hours.

When ready to bake, preheat the oven to 180°C/350°F/Gas Mark 4. Grease a large baking sheet.

Roll out the dough on a lightly floured work surface into a rectangle about 3 mm/$\frac{1}{8}$ inch thick, then use a sharp knife or a biscuit cutter to cut out 24 diamond shapes. Transfer the diamond shapes to the prepared baking sheet. Bake in the preheated oven for 15 minutes, or until golden brown.

Transfer to a wire rack and leave to cool. Dust the biscuits with icing sugar before serving.

CARAWAY BISCUITS

Preheat the oven to 160°C/325°F/Gas Mark 3. Lightly grease 2 large baking sheets.

Sift the flour and salt together into a bowl. Rub in the butter with your fingertips until the mixture resembles fine breadcrumbs. Stir in the caster sugar.

Reserve 1 tablespoon of the beaten egg for brushing the biscuits. Add the remainder of the egg to the mixture along with the caraway seeds and mix to form a soft dough.

Roll out the dough thinly on a lightly floured work surface, then cut out about 36 rounds using a 6-cm/2$\frac{1}{2}$-inch biscuit cutter.

Transfer the rounds to the prepared baking sheets, brush with the reserved egg and sprinkle with demerara sugar.

Bake in the preheated oven for 10–15 minutes, or until lightly golden and crisp.

Transfer to a wire rack and leave to cool. Store in an airtight container.

MAKES 36

85 g/3 oz butter, diced, plus extra
   for greasing
280 g/10 oz plain flour, plus extra
   for dusting
pinch of salt
225 g/8 oz caster sugar
1 egg, beaten
2 tbsp caraway seeds
demerara sugar, for sprinkling

The caraway seed is best known for its appearance in rye bread. Here, caraway seeds give these biscuits a distinctive flavour.

Caraway seeds have a nutty, delicate anise flavour. If you don't like the taste, replace them with poppy seeds.

CHOCOLATE BISCOTTI

Preheat the oven to 180°C/350°F/Gas Mark 4. Lightly grease a large baking sheet.

Using a hand-held electric whisk, beat the egg, sugar and vanilla extract together in a bowl until thick and pale - the mixture should leave a trail when the whisk is lifted.

Sift the flour, baking powder and cinnamon together into a separate bowl, then sift again into the egg mixture and fold in gently. Stir in the chocolate, almonds and pine kernels.

Turn out the dough on a lightly floured work surface and shape into a flat log, measuring 23 cm/9 inches long and 2 cm/^{3}/4 inch wide. Transfer to the prepared baking sheet.

Bake in the preheated oven for 20-25 minutes, or until golden. Leave to cool on the baking sheet for 5 minutes, or until firm.

Transfer the log to a chopping board. Using a serrated bread knife, cut the log diagonally into 16 slices about 1 cm/^{1}/2 inch thick and arrange on the baking sheet. Bake in the oven for a further 10-15

minutes, turning the biscotti onto the other side halfway through the cooking time to bake evenly.

Leave the biscotti to cool on the baking sheet for 5 minutes, then transfer to a wire rack to cool completely.

MAKES 16

butter, for greasing

1 egg

100 g/3^1/2 oz caster sugar

1 tsp vanilla extract

150 g/5^1/2 oz plain flour, plus extra
for dusting

^{1}/2 tsp baking powder

1 tsp ground cinnamon

50 g/1^3/4 oz continental plain
chocolate, roughly chopped

55 g/2 oz toasted flaked almonds

55 g/2 oz pine kernels

Italian-style dry biscuits are a traditional accompaniment to black coffee after dinner, but you may find yourself nibbling them the morning after.

JAMAICAN RUM BISCUITS

Dark rum and coconut lend a deliciously exotic flavour to these biscuits. They are ideal for serving after dinner with coffee.

MAKES 36

175 g/6 oz butter or margarine, plus
    extra for greasing
55 g/2 oz sesame seeds
55 g/2 oz chopped mixed nuts
275 g/9^1/2 oz demerara sugar
1 egg
1 tsp dark rum
140 g/5 oz plain flour
^{1}/4 tsp baking powder
pinch of salt
2 tbsp coconut flakes, to decorate

Preheat the oven to 180°C/350°F/Gas Mark 4. Lightly grease a large baking sheet. Spread the sesame seeds and chopped nuts out on an ungreased baking sheet and toast in the preheated oven for 10 minutes, or until slightly browned. Remove from the oven and set aside.

Cream the butter and sugar together in a bowl until pale and fluffy. Add the egg and rum and beat well. Sift the flour, baking powder and salt together into separate bowl, then beat in the creamed mixture.

Drop 36 rounded teaspoonfuls of the mixture onto the prepared large baking sheet, spaced well apart to allow for spreading. Bake in the oven for 8 minutes, or until golden brown.

Transfer to a wire rack and leave to cool. Decorate with the coconut flakes and serve.

MILLIONAIRE'S SHORTBREAD

MAKES 9

115 g/4 oz butter, diced and chilled,
   plus extra for greasing
225 g/8 oz plain flour
60 g/2¼ oz soft light brown sugar,
   sifted

TOPPING

4 tbsp butter
60 g/2¼ oz soft light brown sugar
500 ml/18 fl oz canned condensed milk
150 g/5½ oz milk chocolate

This rich shortbread topped with
caramel and chocolate makes a special
treat for adults and children alike.

Ensure that the caramel layer is
completely cool and set before coating
it with the melted chocolate, otherwise
they will mix together.

Preheat the oven to 190°C/375°F/Gas Mark 5. Lightly grease a 23-cm/ 9-inch square cake tin.

Sift the flour into a bowl. Rub in the butter with your fingertips until the mixture resembles fine breadcrumbs. Add the sugar and work the mixture to form a firm dough. Don't overwork the shortbread, otherwise it will be tough, not crumbly as it should be.

Lightly press the dough into the base of the prepared tin and prick all over with a fork.

Bake in the preheated oven for 20 minutes, or until firm and lightly golden. Leave to cool in the tin.

To make the topping, put the butter, sugar and condensed milk in a non-stick saucepan over a low heat and cook, stirring constantly, until the mixture comes to the boil.

Reduce the heat and cook for 4–5 minutes, stirring constantly, until the caramel is pale golden and thick, and coming away from the side of the saucepan. Pour the topping over the shortbread and leave to cool.

When the topping is firm, break the chocolate into pieces and melt in a heatproof bowl set over a saucepan of barely simmering water. Spread over the topping and leave to set. Cut into 9 squares to serve.

SHORTBREAD TRIANGLES

MAKES 8

115 g/4 oz butter, diced and chilled, plus extra for greasing

175 g/6 oz plain flour, plus extra for dusting (optional)

pinch of salt

55 g/2 oz caster sugar

2 tsp golden caster sugar

Grease a 20-cm/8-inch round fluted cake tin or flan tin. Preheat the oven to 150°C/300°F/Gas Mark 2.

Sift the flour, salt and caster sugar together into a bowl. Rub in the butter with your fingertips until the mixture resembles fine breadcrumbs. Work the mixture to form a soft dough. Don't overwork the shortbread, otherwise it will be tough, not crumbly as it should be.

Lightly press the dough into the cake tin. If you don't have a fluted tin, roll out the dough on a lightly floured work surface. Transfer to a baking sheet and pinch the edge to form a scalloped pattern.

Mark the dough into 8 equal portions with a knife. Prick all over with a fork and bake in the centre of the preheated oven for 45–50 minutes until firm and lightly golden.

Leave to cool in the tin and dredge with the golden caster sugar. Cut into portions and transfer to a wire rack. Store in an airtight container in a cool place.

Shortbread dates back at least to the 16th century. It is ideal for tea time, coffee in the morning or as an accompaniment to fruit fools or other soft desserts.

The formula for shortbread is usually one part sugar and two parts butter to three parts flour. The sugar used is often caster, the butter slightly salted and the flour plain white, although sometimes a tablespoon of semolina, rice flour or cornflour may replace some of the flour to give a different texture.

BRANDY SNAPS

MAKES 36

oil, for oiling

115 g/4 oz unsalted butter

140 g/5 oz golden syrup

115 g/4 oz demerara sugar

115 g/4 oz plain flour

2 tsp ground ginger

600 ml/1 pint stiffly whipped
   double cream, to serve

If the brandy snaps become too hard before rolling, pop them back in the oven for a few minutes.

Preheat the oven to 160°C/325°F/ Gas Mark 3. Oil a non-stick baking sheet. Heat the butter, syrup and sugar in a saucepan over a low heat, stirring occasionally, until melted and combined. Remove from the heat and leave to cool slightly. Sift the flour and ginger together into the butter mixture and beat until smooth. Spoon 2 teaspoons of the mixture onto the prepared baking sheet, spaced well apart to allow for spreading. Bake in the preheated oven for 8 minutes until pale golden brown. Keep the remaining mixture warm. Meanwhile, oil the handle of a wooden spoon.

Leave to stand on the baking sheet for 1 minute so that the brandy snaps firm up slightly. Remove one with a palette knife and immediately curl it around the handle of the wooden spoon. Once set, carefully slide off the handle and transfer to a wire rack to cool completely. Repeat with the other brandy snap. Bake the remaining mixture on cool baking sheets and shape in the same way. Don't be tempted to cook more than 2 brandy snaps at a time, otherwise the rounds will set before you have time to shape them. When cool, store in an airtight container.

To serve, spoon the cream into a piping bag fitted with a star nozzle. Fill the brandy snaps with cream from both ends.

CHRISTMAS BISCUITS

MAKES ABOUT 24

900 g/2 lb plain flour, plus extra
  for dusting

1 tbsp bicarbonate of soda

1 tbsp ground ginger

3 tsp ground mixed spice

pinch of salt

225 g/8 oz butter or margarine, plus
  extra for greasing

500 g/1 lb 2 oz golden syrup

200 g/7 oz demerara sugar

125 ml/4 fl oz water

1 egg

1 tsp brandy

1 tsp very finely grated orange rind

55 g/2 oz icing sugar, plus extra
  for dusting

These festive biscuits will quickly
become an annual favourite. Store
them in an airtight container for up
to a week.

Sift the flour, bicarbonate of soda, ginger, mixed spice and salt together into a bowl. Beat the butter, syrup, demerara sugar, water, egg and brandy together in a separate bowl until thoroughly combined. Gradually stir in the orange rind, then the flour mixture.

Halve the dough, wrap in clingfilm and chill in the refrigerator for at least 4 hours (it will keep for up to 6 days).

When ready to bake, preheat the oven to 180°C/350°F/Gas Mark 4. Grease a baking sheet. Roll each half of dough into a ball on a lightly floured work surface, then roll out to a thickness of 3 mm/^{1}/8 inch. Cut out about 24 festive shapes such as stars and Christmas trees using biscuit cutters or a knife. Transfer to the prepared baking sheet. Bake in the preheated oven for 10 minutes, or until golden brown. Transfer to a wire rack and leave to cool.

When the biscuits have cooled, mix the icing sugar with a little water in a small bowl. Drizzle the icing over some of the biscuits and dust the remainder with sifted icing sugar.

CHOCOLATE CHIP BISCUITS

No chocolate-loving cook's repertoire would be complete without a chocolate chip biscuit recipe. This recipe can be used to make several different varieties (see below).

MAKES 18

215 g/7$^{1}/_{2}$ oz plain flour, sifted

1 tsp baking powder

115 g/4 oz soft margarine, plus extra for greasing

125 g/4$^{1}/_{2}$ oz soft light brown sugar

50 g/1$^{3}/_{4}$ oz caster sugar

$^{1}/_{2}$ tsp vanilla extract

1 egg

115 g/4 oz plain chocolate chips

Preheat the oven to 190°C/375°F/Gas Mark 5. Lightly grease 2 baking sheets. Put all the ingredients in a large bowl and beat well until thoroughly combined.

Drop 18 tablespoonfuls of the mixture onto the prepared baking sheets, spaced well apart to allow for spreading.

Bake in the preheated oven for 10-12 minutes until golden brown. Using a spatula, transfer the biscuits to a wire rack to cool completely before serving.

For Choc and Nut Biscuits, add 85 g/3 oz chopped hazelnuts to the basic mixture. For Double Choc Biscuits, beat in 40 g/1$^{1}/_{2}$ oz melted plain chocolate. For White Chocolate Chip Biscuits, use white chocolate chips instead of the plain chocolate chips.

LEMON DROPS

MAKES 24

115 g/4 oz butter or margarine, plus
   extra for greasing

200 g/7 oz caster sugar

2 tbsp lemon juice

1 tbsp finely grated lemon rind

2 tbsp water

225 g/8 oz plain flour, sifted

1 tsp bicarbonate of soda

1/2 tsp cream of tartar

TO DECORATE

icing sugar

crystallized fruit, chopped finely
   (optional)

Preheat the oven to 180°C/350°F/Gas Mark 4. Grease a large baking sheet. Beat together the butter, caster sugar, lemon juice, lemon rind and water.

In a separate bowl, mix together the flour, bicarbonate of soda and cream of tartar. Add the butter mixture and blend together well.

Spoon the mixture into a piping bag fitted with a star-shaped nozzle. Pipe 24 fancy drops, about the size of a tablespoon, onto the greased baking sheet, allowing room for the biscuits to spread during cooking. Transfer to the preheated oven and bake for 10 minutes, or until the lemon drops are golden brown.

Remove from the oven, then transfer to a wire rack and leave to cool completely. Dust with icing sugar and sprinkle over the crystallized fruit, if liked.

Serve these with lemon tea,
sweetened with a little honey if liked.
They also make a delicious dessert.

small cakes AND *pastries*

There is nothing so satisfying as creating a tray of little baked delights. This chapter is a celebration of the small cake and its comfortingly indulgent cousin – the pastry. There is a tiny treat for every occasion – from children's birthdays to afternoon snacks, from the classic cupcake, to the empanada, a sweet-filled pastry crust. Whether adorned with silver balls, or shaped into pastry nests, the young and the young at heart will love these tantalizing treats.

CUP CAKES

Preheat the oven to 180°C/350°F/Gas Mark 4. Line 2 muffin tins with 20 muffin paper cases.

Put the water, butter, caster sugar and syrup in a saucepan over a low heat and heat, stirring, until the sugar has dissolved. Increase the heat and bring to the boil. Reduce the heat and cook gently for 5 minutes. Remove from the heat and leave to cool. Put the milk and vanilla extract in a bowl. Add the bicarbonate of soda and stir to dissolve. Sift the cocoa powder and flour into a separate bowl and add the syrup mixture. Stir in the milk mixture and beat until smooth.

Carefully spoon the mixture into the paper cases to come within two-thirds of the tops. Bake in the preheated oven for 20 minutes, or until well risen and firm to the touch. Transfer to a wire rack and leave to cool.

To make the icing, melt the plain chocolate in a small heatproof bowl with half the water and half the butter set over a saucepan of barely simmering water. Stir until smooth and leave to stand over the water. Repeat with the white chocolate and remaining water and butter.

Stir half the icing sugar into each bowl and beat until smooth and fudgy. Divide the icings between the cakes, filling to the tops of the paper cases. Leave to cool, then place a rose petal on each plain chocolate-iced cake and a violet on each white chocolate-iced cake. Leave to set before serving.

These pretty little cakes are light and moist, with a tempting fudgy chocolate topping - perfect for serving at any time of the day.

Instead of the crystallized flower petals, the cakes could be decorated with chocolate curls or chopped hazelnuts.

MAKES 20

200 ml/7 fl oz water

85 g/3 oz butter

85 g/3 oz caster sugar

1 tbsp golden syrup

3 tbsp milk

1 tsp vanilla extract

1 tsp bicarbonate of soda

2 tbsp cocoa powder

225 g/8 oz plain flour

ICING

50 g/1³/4 oz plain chocolate, broken into pieces

4 tbsp water

50 g/1³/4 oz butter

50 g/1³/4 oz white chocolate, broken into pieces

350 g/12 oz icing sugar

TO DECORATE

crystallized rose petals

crystallized violets

LAVENDER FAIRY CAKES

MAKES 12

115 g/4 oz golden caster sugar

115 g/4 oz butter, softened

2 eggs, beaten

1 tbsp milk

1 tsp finely chopped lavender flowers

1/2 tsp vanilla extract

175 g/6 oz self-raising flour, sifted

140 g/5 oz icing sugar

TO DECORATE

lavender flowers

silver dragées

Preheat the oven to 200°C/400°F/Gas Mark 6. Line a 12-hole bun tin with cake paper cases.

Cream the caster sugar and butter together in a bowl until pale and fluffy. Gradually beat in the eggs. Stir in the milk, chopped lavender flowers and vanilla extract, then gently fold in the flour.

Divide the mixture between the paper cases and bake in the preheated oven for 12-15 minutes, or until well risen, golden and springy to the touch. A few minutes before the cakes are ready, sift the icing sugar into a bowl. Stir in enough water to make a thick icing.

Transfer the cakes to a wire rack. Add a blob of icing to the centre of each, allowing it to run across the cake. Decorate with lavender flowers and silver dragées. Serve when cool.

Lavender might seem like an unusual ingredient, but it gives a special fragrance and flavour to these little cakes. Add a little purple food colouring to the icing to give it a pale lilac colour to complement the lavender.

Always make sure that your lavender flowers are suitable to eat and free from any chemical sprays or insecticides.

COCONUT FLAPJACKS

Freshly baked, these chewy flapjacks are always a favourite for after-school snacks and just the thing for tea time.

The flapjacks are best stored in an airtight container and eaten within a week. They can also be frozen for up to 1 month. Make sure that they are thawed before eating.

MAKES 16

200 g/7 oz butter, plus extra
for greasing
200 g/7 oz demerara sugar
2 tbsp golden syrup
275 g/9½ oz porridge oats
100 g/3½ oz desiccated coconut
75 g/2¾ oz glacé cherries, chopped

Preheat the oven to 160ºC/325ºF/Gas Mark 3. Grease a 30 x 23 cm/ 12 x 9 inch baking tray.

Put the butter, sugar and syrup in a large saucepan over a low heat and heat until just melted. Stir in the oats, coconut and cherries and mix until thoroughly combined.

Spread the mixture evenly into the prepared baking tray and press down with the back of a spatula to make a smooth surface.

Bake in the preheated oven for 30 minutes. Leave to cool in the baking tray for 10 minutes. Cut the flapjack into 16 rectangles using a sharp knife. Carefully transfer the pieces of flapjack to a wire rack and leave to cool completely.

WALNUT PASTRIES

These delicious pastries can be eaten as an afternoon snack or on special occasions.

MAKES 12

100 g/3¹/₂ oz butter

350 g/12 oz walnut pieces, finely chopped

55 g/2 oz caster sugar

1 tsp ground cinnamon

¹/₂ tsp ground cloves

225 g/8 oz filo pastry

225 g/8 oz honey

2 tsp lemon juice

150 ml/5 fl oz water

Preheat the oven to 220°C/425°F/Gas Mark 7. Put the butter in a saucepan over a low heat and heat until just melted. Use a little to lightly grease a deep 25 x 18-cm/10 x 7-inch roasting tin.

To make the filling, put the walnuts, sugar, cinnamon and cloves in a bowl and mix together well.

Cut the pastry sheets in half widthways. Take a sheet of pastry and use to line the tin. Cover the remaining sheets with a damp tea towel. Brush the sheet with a little of the melted butter. Repeat with half the pastry sheets, then sprinkle over the walnut filling. Top with the remaining pastry sheets, brushing each with melted butter and tucking down the edges.

Using a sharp knife, cut the top layers of the pastry into 12 diamond or square shapes.

Bake the pastry in the preheated oven for 10 minutes, then reduce the oven temperature to 180°C/350°F/Gas Mark 4 and bake for a further 20 minutes, or until golden brown.

Just before the pastry is ready, put the honey, lemon juice and water in a saucepan over a medium heat and simmer for 5 minutes, or until well combined. Set aside.

Remove the pastry from the oven and pour the honey mixture evenly over it. Leave to cool. To serve, cut along the marked lines again to divide into pieces.

ORANGE AND WALNUT CAKES

Preheat the oven to 180°C/350°F/Gas Mark 4. Sift the flour, bicarbonate of soda, cinnamon, cloves, nutmeg and salt together into a bowl. Beat the oil and sugar together in a separate bowl. Add the orange rind and juice, then gradually beat in the flour mixture.

Turn out the dough onto a lightly floured surface and knead for 2-3 minutes until smooth.

Break off egg-sized pieces of dough and shape into ovals. Transfer to baking trays, spaced well apart to allow for spreading. Using the back of a fork, press the top of each twice to create a criss-cross design.

Bake the cakes in the preheated oven for 20 minutes, or until lightly browned. Transfer to a wire rack and leave to cool.

Meanwhile, to make the topping, mix the walnuts and cinnamon together in a small bowl. To make the syrup, put the honey and water in a saucepan and bring to the boil. Reduce the heat and simmer for 5 minutes. Remove from the heat and add the lemon and orange juices and brandy.

When the cakes are almost cool, using a slotted spoon, submerge each cake in the hot syrup and leave for about 1 minute. Put on a tray and top each with some of the walnut mixture. Leave to cool completely before serving.

MAKES ABOUT 18

400 g/14 oz self-raising flour, plus extra for dusting

1/2 tsp bicarbonate of soda

1/2 tsp ground cinnamon

1/4 tsp ground cloves

pinch of freshly grated nutmeg

pinch of salt

150 ml/5 fl oz olive oil

75 g/2 3/4 oz caster sugar

finely grated rind and juice of 1 large orange

TOPPING

25 g/1 oz walnut pieces, finely chopped

1/2 tsp ground cinnamon

SYRUP

175 g/6 oz honey

125 ml/4 fl oz water

juice of 1 small lemon

juice of 1 small orange

2 tbsp brandy

These delicately spiced orange-flavoured cakes are festive treats. After baking, they are dipped in a hot honey syrup and sprinkled with chopped walnuts. They are intensely sweet, but you can omit the syrup if you don't think it will suit your taste.

MERINGUES

These are just as meringues should be - as light as air and at the same time crisp and melt-in-the-mouth. Store in an airtight container.

For a finer texture, replace the granulated sugar with caster sugar.

MAKES 13

4 egg whites

pinch of salt

115 g/4 oz granulated sugar

115 g/4 oz caster sugar

300 ml/10 fl oz double cream,
  lightly whipped

Preheat the oven to 120°C/250°F/Gas Mark $^1/2$. Line 3 baking sheets with non-stick baking paper.

Using a hand-held electric whisk or balloon whisk, beat the egg whites and salt together in a large, clean bowl until stiff - you should be able to turn the bowl upside down without the egg whites moving.

Whisk in the granulated sugar, a little at a time - the meringue should start to look glossy at this stage.

Sprinkle in the caster sugar, a little at a time, and continue whisking until all the sugar has been incorporated and the meringue is thick, white and stands in tall peaks.

Transfer the meringue mixture to a piping bag fitted with a 2-cm/$^3/4$-inch star nozzle. Pipe 26 small whirls onto the prepared baking sheets.

Bake in the preheated oven for 1$^1/2$ hours, or until the meringues are pale golden in colour and can be easily lifted off the paper. Turn off the oven and leave the meringues inside overnight.

Just before serving, sandwich the meringues together in pairs with the whipped cream and arrange on a serving plate.

PEACH AND PECAN EMPANADAS

MAKES 8

350 g/12 oz ready-made puff pastry,
    thawed if frozen

plain flour, for dusting

3 fresh ripe peaches

150 ml/5 fl oz soured cream

4 tbsp soft light brown sugar

4 tbsp pecan halves, toasted and
    finely chopped

beaten egg, for sealing and glazing

caster sugar, for sprinkling

These sweet empanadas have a
creamy, fruity filling and a hint of
crunchy nut. You could use
apricots or mangoes in place of the
peaches, adding some extra slices of
fruit to decorate. Serve as a snack
or a dessert.

Preheat the oven to 200°C/400°F/Gas Mark 6. Roll out the pastry on a lightly floured work surface. Using a 15-cm/6-inch saucer as a guide, cut out 8 rounds.

Cut a small cross in the stem end of each peach. Lower into a saucepan of boiling water and leave to stand for 30 seconds. Drain and cool under cold running water. Using a small, sharp knife, peel, then halve the peaches. Remove the stones and slice the flesh.

Put a spoonful of soured cream in the centre of a pastry round and top with a few peach slices. Sprinkle over a little brown sugar and some nuts. Brush each edge with a little beaten egg, fold the pastry over the filling and press the edges together to seal. Crimp the edges with the tines of a fork and prick the tops.

Transfer to a baking sheet, brush with beaten egg and sprinkle with caster sugar. Bake in the preheated oven for 20 minutes, or until golden brown. Serve warm.

ECCLES CAKES

Preheat the oven to 220ºC/425ºF/Gas Mark 7. Grease a baking sheet.

Roll out the pastry thinly on a lightly floured work surface. Using a 9-cm/3½-inch plain pastry cutter, cut out 10-12 rounds.

Cream the butter and brown sugar together in a bowl until pale and fluffy, then beat in the currants, mixed peel and mixed spice, if using.

Put a teaspoon of the filling in the centre of each pastry round. Draw the edge of each round together and pinch over the filling. Reshape each cake into a round.

Turn the cakes over and lightly roll them with the rolling pin until the currants just show through. Score with a knife into a lattice pattern.

Transfer the cakes to the prepared baking sheet and leave to rest for 10-15 minutes.

Brush the cakes with the egg white, sprinkle with the caster sugar and bake at the top of the preheated oven for 15 minutes, or until golden brown and crisp.

Transfer to a wire rack and sprinkle with a little more sugar, if you like. Serve immediately or leave to cool completely and store in an airtight container for up to 1 week. The cakes can be reheated before serving.

MAKES 10-12

400 g/14 oz ready-made puff pastry, thawed if frozen

plain flour, for dusting

55 g/2 oz butter, softened, plus extra for greasing

55 g/2 oz soft light brown sugar

85 g/3 oz currants

25 g/1 oz mixed peel, chopped

½ tsp ground mixed spice (optional)

1 egg white, lightly beaten

1 tsp caster sugar, plus extra for sprinkling (optional)

These cakes originated from cooks using up leftover foods, which were enveloped in pastry so they could be baked or fried. The filling can be any leftover fruit mixed with butter, brown sugar, and spice.

CHERRY AND SULTANA ROCK CAKES

Rock cakes are always popular and they are very quick and easy to make. To be at their best, they should be eaten the day they are made.

MAKES 10

85 g/3 oz butter, diced and chilled, plus extra for greasing

250 g/9 oz self-raising flour

1 tsp ground mixed spice

85 g/3 oz golden caster sugar

55 g/2 oz glacé cherries, quartered

55 g/2 oz sultanas

1 egg

2 tbsp milk

demerara sugar, for sprinkling

Preheat the oven to 200°C/400°F/Gas Mark 6. Lightly grease a baking sheet. Sift the flour and mixed spice together into a bowl. Rub in the butter with your fingertips until the mixture resembles fine breadcrumbs. Stir in the caster sugar, cherries and sultanas.

Break the egg into a bowl and whisk in the milk. Pour most of the egg mixture into the dry ingredients and mix with a fork to form a stiff, coarse dough, adding the remainder of the egg mixture if necessary.

Using 2 forks, pile the dough into 10 rocky heaps on the prepared baking sheet. Sprinkle with demerara sugar.

Bake in the preheated oven for 10-15 minutes, or until golden and firm to the touch. Leave to cool on the baking sheet for 2 minutes, then transfer to a wire rack and leave to cool completely.

PAPER-THIN FRUIT PIES

Preheat the oven to 200°C/400°F/Gas Mark 6. Put the butter in a small saucepan over a low heat and heat until just melted. Brush 4 holes of a non-stick muffin tin, 10 cm/4 inches in diameter, with a little of the melted butter.

Core and thinly slice the apple and pear, then immediately toss them in the lemon juice to prevent them turning brown.

Cut each sheet of pastry into 4 and cover with a clean, damp tea towel. Working on each pie separately, brush 4 small sheets of pastry with the melted butter. Press a pastry sheet into the base of one prepared hole. Arrange the other pastry sheets on top at slightly different angles. Repeat with the remaining pastry to make another 3 pies.

Arrange the apple and pear slices alternately in the centre of each pie case and lightly crimp the edge of the pastry of each pie.

Stir the jam and orange juice together in a small bowl until smooth, then brush over the fruit. Bake in the preheated oven for 12-15 minutes. Sprinkle with the pistachio nuts, dust lightly with icing sugar and serve hot from the oven with custard.

SERVES 4

55 g/2 oz butter or margarine

1 eating apple

1 ripe pear

2 tbsp lemon juice

4 sheets filo pastry, thawed if frozen

2 tbsp apricot jam

1 tbsp orange juice

1 tbsp finely chopped pistachio nuts

2 tsp icing sugar, for dusting

custard, to serve

These extra-crisp filo pastry cases, filled with slices of fresh fruit and glazed with apricot jam, are a delicious low-fat treat.

BANANA CREAM PROFITEROLES

SERVES 4

DOUGH

5 tbsp butter, diced, plus extra
  for greasing

150 ml/5 fl oz water, plus extra
  for sprinkling

85 g/3 oz strong plain flour, sifted

2 eggs

CHOCOLATE SAUCE

100 g /3^{1}/2 oz plain chocolate, broken
  into pieces

2 tbsp water

4 tbsp icing sugar

2 tbsp butter

FILLING

300 ml/10 fl oz double cream

1 banana, peeled

2 tbsp icing sugar

2 tbsp crème de banane

Preheat the oven to 220°C/425°F/Gas Mark 7. Lightly grease a baking sheet and sprinkle with a little water.

To make the dough, put the water and butter in a saucepan over a low heat and heat until the butter has melted. Bring to a rolling boil. Remove from the heat and add the flour, all at once, beating well until the mixture leaves the side of the saucepan and forms a ball. Leave to cool slightly. Gradually beat in the eggs until the dough is smooth and glossy.

Spoon the paste into a large piping bag fitted with a 1-cm/^{1}/2-inch plain nozzle.

Pipe about 18 small balls of the paste onto the prepared baking sheet, spaced well apart to allow for spreading. Bake in the preheated oven for 15–20 minutes until crisp and golden. Make a small slit in each one for the steam to escape, then transfer to a wire rack and leave to cool.

Meanwhile, to make the sauce, put all the sauce ingredients in a heatproof bowl set over a saucepan of barely simmering water and heat, stirring constantly, until combined and smooth.

To make the filling, whip the cream in a bowl until soft peaks form. Mash the banana with the icing sugar and liqueur in a separate bowl. Fold into the cream. Transfer the filling to a piping bag fitted with a 1-cm/^{1}/2-inch plain nozzle. Pipe the filling into the profiteroles. Serve with the hot sauce poured over.

Chocolate profiteroles are a popular choice. In this recipe, they are filled with a delicious banana-flavoured cream - the perfect combination!

CHOCOLATE BUTTERFLY CAKES

Filled with a tangy lemon buttercream, these appealing little cakes will become an all-time favourite with both adults and children.

For a chocolate buttercream, beat the butter and icing sugar together, then beat in 25 g/1 oz melted plain chocolate.

MAKES 12

115 g/4 oz soft margarine

100 g/3¹/₂ oz caster sugar

225 g/8 oz self-raising flour

2 large eggs

2 tbsp cocoa powder

25 g/1 oz plain chocolate, melted

icing sugar, for dusting

LEMON BUTTERCREAM

85 g/3 oz butter, preferably unsalted, softened

150 g/5¹/₂ oz icing sugar, sifted

grated rind of ¹/₂ lemon

1 tbsp lemon juice

Preheat the oven to 180°C/350°F/Gas Mark 4. Line a shallow 12-hole muffin tin with muffin paper cases.

Put all the cake ingredients, except the melted chocolate and icing sugar, in a large bowl. Using a hand-held electric whisk, beat until the mixture is just smooth. Beat in the melted chocolate.

Divide the mixture equally between the paper cases, filling each three-quarters full. Bake in the preheated oven for 15 minutes, or until springy to the touch. Transfer to a wire rack and leave to cool.

Meanwhile, to make the lemon buttercream, beat the butter in a bowl until pale and fluffy, then gradually beat in the icing sugar. Beat in the lemon rind, then gradually add the lemon juice, beating well.

When cool, using a serrated knife, cut the top off each cake. Cut each cake top in half. Spread or pipe the buttercream over the cut surface of each cake and push the 2 cut pieces of cake top into the icing to form wings. Dust with icing sugar.

CHOCOLATE HAZELNUT PALMIERS

MAKES 26

butter, for greasing

375 g/13 oz ready-made puff pastry,
   thawed if frozen

plain flour, for dusting

8 tbsp chocolate hazelnut spread

75 g/2³/₄ oz chopped toasted
   hazelnuts

2 tbsp caster sugar

Preheat the oven to 220°C/425°F/Gas Mark 7. Grease a baking sheet. Roll out the pastry on a lightly floured work surface into a rectangle about 38 x 23 cm/15 x 9 inches.

Spread the chocolate hazelnut spread over the pastry using a palette knife, then scatter the hazelnuts over the top.

Roll up one long side of the pastry to the centre, then the other, so that they meet in the centre. Where the pieces meet, dampen the edges with a little water to join them. Using a sharp knife, cut into 26 thin slices. Transfer each slice to the prepared baking sheet and flatten slightly with a palette knife. Sprinkle with the sugar.

Bake in the preheated oven for 10-15 minutes, or until golden. Transfer to a wire rack and leave to cool.

These delicious chocolate and hazelnut biscuits are very simple to make, yet so effective. For very young children, leave out the chopped nuts.

MOCHA **ROLLS**

Preheat the oven to 180°C/350°F/Gas Mark 4. For the sponge cake, base-line a 30 x 20 x 4-cm/12 x 8 x 1¹/2-inch rectangular cake tin with non-stick baking paper. Put the eggs, egg white and sugar in a heatproof bowl, set over a saucepan of barely simmering water and whisk until thick and pale. Remove from the heat, then whisk until cool. Sift over the flour and fold in. Fold in the melted butter, a little at a time.

Pour the mixture into the prepared tin and bake in the preheated oven for 25–30 minutes until the cake is springy to the touch and has shrunk slightly from the sides of the tin. Remove from the oven and transfer to a wire rack, still standing on the lining paper, to cool.

Meanwhile, put 2 tablespoons of the coffee into a small heatproof bowl and sprinkle the gelatine on the surface. Leave to soften for 2 minutes, then set the bowl over a saucepan of barely simmering water and stir until the gelatine has dissolved. Remove from the heat. Put the remaining coffee, liqueur and ricotta cheese in a food processor or blender and process until smooth. Add the gelatine mixture in a continuous stream and process briefly. Scrape the mixture into a bowl, cover with clingfilm and chill in the refrigerator for 1–1¹/2 hours until set.

Peel the lining paper off the cake. Using a knife, cut the cake in half horizontally. Trim off any dried edges. Cut each piece of cake in half lengthways. Put each piece between 2 sheets of baking paper and roll with a rolling pin to make it more flexible. Spread one side of each cake piece with a 5-mm/¹/4-inch thick layer of the coffee filling, leaving a 5-mm/¹/4-inch margin all round. Cut each strip across into 4 pieces, to give a total of 16. Roll up each piece from the short end, like a Swiss roll.

Put one roll seam-side down on a metal palette knife and hold it over the bowl of melted white chocolate. Spoon the chocolate over the roll to coat. Transfer to a sheet of baking paper. Repeat with the remaining rolls.

Spoon the plain chocolate into a greaseproof paper piping bag fitted with a small, plain nozzle and pipe zig-zags along the rolls. Leave to set.

MAKES 16

150 ml/5 fl oz cold strong black coffee

1 tbsp gelatine

1 tsp Kahlúa or other coffee-flavoured liqueur

225 g/8 oz ricotta cheese

280 g/10 oz white chocolate, melted

25 g/1 oz plain chocolate, melted

SPONGE CAKE

3 eggs, plus 1 egg white

85 g/3 oz caster sugar

100 g/3¹/2 oz plain flour

2 tbsp butter, melted

Plain and white chocolate are combined with coffee and Kahlúa in these attractive sponge-cake rolls.

RASPBERRY CHOCOLATE ECLAIRS

These small éclairs are perfect for serving at a summer tea party. They look particularly appealing arranged on a pretty serving plate.

MAKES 20-24

150 ml/5 fl oz water

55 g/2 oz butter

70 g/2¹/2 oz plain flour, sifted

2 eggs, beaten

FILLING AND TOPPING

175 ml/6 fl oz double cream

1 tbsp icing sugar

175 g/6 oz fresh raspberries

85 g/3 oz plain chocolate,
   melted

Preheat the oven to 220°C/425°F/Gas Mark 7. Sprinkle 2 baking sheets with a little water. Put the water and butter in a saucepan over a low heat and heat until the butter has melted. Bring to a rolling boil. Remove from the heat and add the flour, all at once, beating well until the mixture leaves the side of the saucepan and forms a ball. Leave to cool slightly. Gradually beat in the eggs until the dough is smooth and glossy.

Spoon into a piping bag fitted with a 1-cm/¹/2-inch plain nozzle. Pipe 20-24 x 7.5-cm/3-inch lengths onto the prepared baking sheets, spaced well apart to allow for spreading. Bake in the preheated oven for 10 minutes. Reduce the temperature to 190°C/375°F/Gas Mark 5 and bake for a further 20 minutes, or until crisp and golden. Split each éclair for the steam to escape, then transfer to a wire rack and leave to cool.

To make the filling, whip the cream and sugar together in a bowl until thick. Spoon into the éclairs. Put a few raspberries in each éclair. Spread a little melted chocolate on each éclair and leave to set before serving.

COCONUT AND CHERRY CAKES

Preheat the oven to 180°C/350°F/Gas Mark 4. Line 1 or 2 muffin tins with 8 muffin paper cases. Cream the butter and sugar together in a bowl until pale and fluffy, then stir in the milk.

Gradually beat in the eggs. Sift in the flour and baking powder and fold in with the coconut. Gently fold in most of the cherries. Spoon the mixture into the paper cases and scatter the remaining cherries on top.

Bake in the preheated oven for 20-25 minutes, or until well risen, golden and springy to the touch. Transfer to a wire rack and leave to cool.

MAKES 8

115 g/4 oz butter, softened

115 g/4 oz golden caster sugar

2 tbsp milk

2 eggs, beaten

85 g/3 oz self-raising flour

1/2 tsp baking powder

85 g/3 oz desiccated coconut

115 g/4 oz glacé cherries, quartered

Coconut and glacé cherries make these little cakes really moist, and give them a sweet flavour that will make them a hit with children.

family cakes
AND *tray bakes*

Everyone has his or her favourite family cake. It can be the cake that evokes memories of munching happily in a cosy kitchen surrounded by the sweet aroma of baking, or simply the cake that can be depended on time and time again to cheer up your day with the first mouthful. From the classic Victoria Sandwich to Moist Chocolate Cake, this chapter contains a collection of cakes and bakes that provide the perfect starting point for beginners.

VICTORIA SANDWICH

Preheat the oven to 180ºC/350ºF/Gas Mark 4. Grease 2 x 20-cm/8-inch round shallow cake tins and base-line with greaseproof or non-stick baking paper.

Cream the butter and sugar together in a bowl until pale and fluffy. Add the eggs, a little at a time, beating well after each addition.

Sift the flour and salt together, then gently fold into the mixture using a metal spoon or a spatula. Divide the mixture between the prepared tins and smooth the surfaces.

Bake both cakes on the same shelf in the centre of the preheated oven for 25–30 minutes until well risen, golden brown and beginning to shrink from the side of each tin.

Leave to stand in the tins for 1 minute. Using a palette knife, loosen the cakes from around the edge of each tin. Turn out the cakes onto a clean tea towel, remove the lining paper and invert onto a wire rack (this prevents the wire rack from marking the top of the cakes).

When completely cool, sandwich together with the jam and sprinkle with the sugar. The cake is delicious when freshly baked, but any remaining cake can be stored in an airtight tin for up to 1 week.

MAKES 8-10 SLICES

175 g/6 oz butter, at room
temperature, plus extra for greasing

175 g/6 oz caster sugar

3 eggs, beaten

175 g/6 oz self-raising flour

pinch of salt

TO SERVE

3 tbsp raspberry jam

1 tbsp caster or icing sugar

This cake is traditionally made by the creaming method, although you can easily make it by the all-in-one method – just make sure that the butter is softened, add 1 teaspoon of baking powder to the flour and then beat all the ingredients together with an electric mixer. It makes a useful base for a child's birthday cake.

UPSIDE-DOWN PUDDING

SERVES 6-8

225 g/8 oz unsalted butter, plus extra
    for greasing

55 g/2 oz soft light brown sugar

14-16 hazelnuts

600 g/1 lb 5 oz canned apricot halves,
    drained

175 g/6 oz demerara sugar

3 eggs, beaten

175 g/6 oz self-raising flour

55 g/2 oz ground hazelnuts

2 tbsp milk

custard or thick cream, to serve

Sometimes known as an 'upside-down
cake', this is a creamed cake mixture
that is baked with fruit under it, so
that when it is turned out, the fruit is
on top and looks decorative. It has a
lovely rich butter and sugar topping as
well, which gives the pudding an
attractive, glossy appearance. You
could use pear halves with walnuts
instead of apricots and hazelnuts.

Preheat the oven to 180°C/350°F/Gas Mark 4. Grease a 25-cm/10-inch round cake tin and base-line with non-stick baking paper.

Cream 55 g/2 oz of the butter and the soft light brown sugar together in a bowl until pale and fluffy. Spread over the base of the prepared tin. Put a hazelnut in each apricot half and invert onto the base. The apricots should cover the whole surface.

Cream the remaining butter and the demerara sugar in a bowl until pale and fluffy. Add the eggs, a little at a time, beating well after each addition. Sift the flour, then gently fold into the mixture with the hazelnuts and milk using a metal spoon or a spatula. Spread the mixture over the apricots.

Bake in the centre of the preheated oven for 45 minutes, or until golden brown and well risen. Run a knife round the edge of the pudding and invert onto a warmed plate. Serve warm with custard or cream.

BANANA AND CRANBERRY LOAF

Preheat the oven to 180°C/350°F/Gas Mark 4. Grease a 900-g/2-lb loaf tin and base-line with non-stick baking paper.

Sift the flour and baking powder together into a bowl. Stir in the brown sugar, bananas, mixed peel, nuts and dried cranberries.

Stir the orange juice, eggs and oil together in a separate bowl until well combined. Add the mixture to the dry ingredients and mix until thoroughly blended. Spoon the mixture into the prepared loaf tin and smooth the surface.

Bake in the preheated oven for 1 hour, or until firm to the touch or a skewer inserted into the centre of the loaf comes out clean.

Turn out the loaf onto a wire rack and leave to cool.

Mix the icing sugar with a little water in a small bowl and drizzle the icing over the loaf. Sprinkle the orange rind over the top. Leave the icing to set before slicing and serving.

SERVES 8

butter, for greasing

225 g/8 oz self-raising flour

1/2 tsp baking powder

125 g/4 1/2 oz soft light brown sugar

2 bananas, peeled and mashed

50 g/1 3/4 oz mixed peel

40 g/1 1/2 oz chopped mixed nuts

70 g/2 1/2 oz dried cranberries

5–6 tbsp orange juice

2 eggs, beaten

150 ml/5 fl oz sunflower oil

85 g/3 oz icing sugar, sifted

grated rind of 1 orange

The addition of chopped nuts, candied peel, fresh orange juice and dried cranberries makes this a rich, moist teabread.

This teabread will keep for a couple of days. Wrap it carefully and store in a cool, dry place.

RASPBERRY DESSERT CAKE

SERVES 9–10

250 g/9 oz plain chocolate, broken
   into pieces

225 g/8 oz unsalted butter, plus extra
   for greasing

1 tbsp strong, dark coffee

5 eggs

100 g/3$\frac{1}{2}$ oz golden caster sugar

85 g/3 oz plain flour

1 tsp ground cinnamon

175 g/6 oz fresh raspberries, plus
   extra to serve

icing sugar, for dusting

whipped cream, to serve

Preheat the oven to 160ºC/325ºF/Gas Mark 3. Grease a 23-cm/9-inch cake tin and line the base with non-stick baking paper. Put the chocolate, butter and coffee in a small, heatproof bowl, set the bowl over a saucepan of barely simmering water and heat until melted. Remove from the heat, stir and leave to cool slightly.

Beat the eggs and caster sugar together in a separate bowl until pale and thick. Gently fold in the chocolate mixture.

Sift the flour and cinnamon into another bowl, then fold into the chocolate mixture. Pour into the prepared tin and sprinkle the raspberries evenly over the top.

Bake in the preheated oven for about 35-45 minutes, or until the cake is well risen and springy to the touch. Leave to cool in the tin for 15 minutes before turning out on to a large serving plate. Dust with icing sugar before serving with extra fresh raspberries and whipped cream.

If fresh raspberries are not available, frozen raspberries may be used. Since these will be softer than fresh fruit, take care to thaw them thoroughly and drain off any excess juice.

CHOCOLATE CHIP BROWNIES

Choose a good-quality plain chocolate for these chocolate chip brownies to give them a rich flavour that is not too sweet. The brownie won't be completely firm in the centre when it is removed from the oven, but it will set when it has cooled.

MAKES 12

225 g/8 oz butter, softened, plus extra for greasing

150 g/5^1/$_2$ oz plain chocolate, broken into pieces

280 g/10 oz plain flour

100 g/3^1/$_2$ oz caster sugar

4 eggs, beaten

75 g/2^3/$_4$ oz chopped pistachio nuts

100 g/3^1/$_2$ oz white chocolate, roughly chopped

icing sugar, for dusting

Preheat the oven to 180°C/350°F/Gas Mark 4. Lightly grease a 23-cm/9-inch square baking tin and line with greaseproof paper.

Melt the plain chocolate and butter in a heatproof bowl set over a saucepan of barely simmering water. Leave to cool slightly.

Sift the flour into a separate bowl and stir in the caster sugar.

Stir the eggs into the melted chocolate mixture, then pour this mixture into the flour mixture, beating well. Stir in the pistachio nuts and white chocolate, then pour the mixture into the tin, spreading it evenly into the corners.

Bake in the preheated oven for 30–35 minutes until firm to the touch. Leave to cool in the tin for 20 minutes, then turn out onto a wire rack.

Leave to cool completely, then cut into 12 pieces and dust with icing sugar.

STRAWBERRY ROULADE

3 large eggs

115 g/4 oz caster sugar

115 g/4 oz plain flour

1 tbsp hot water

FILLING

175 g/6 oz mascarpone cheese

1 tsp almond extract

225 g/8 oz small strawberries

TO DECORATE

1 tbsp flaked almonds, toasted

1 tsp icing sugar

Serve this moist, light sponge cake rolled up with a creamy almond and strawberry filling for a delicious tea-time treat.

Preheat the oven to 220°C/425°F/Gas Mark 7. Line a 35-x-25-cm/14-x-10-inch Swiss roll tin with non-stick baking paper.

Put the eggs and caster sugar in a heatproof bowl set over a saucepan of barely simmering water. Using a hand-held electric whisk, beat together until thick and pale – the mixture should leave a trail when the whisk is lifted.

Remove the bowl from the saucepan. Sift in the flour and fold into the egg mixture with the hot water. Pour the mixture into the prepared tin and bake in the preheated oven for 8-10 minutes until golden and set.

Turn out the cake onto a sheet of non-stick baking paper. Peel off the lining paper and roll up the sponge cake tightly, encasing the baking paper. Wrap in a clean tea towel and leave to cool.

Mix the mascarpone and almond extract together. Reserving a few strawberries for decoration, wash, hull and slice the remainder. Chill with the mascarpone mixture in the refrigerator until required.

Unroll the cake, spread with the mascarpone mixture and sprinkle with sliced strawberries. Roll the cake up again and transfer to a serving plate. Sprinkle with the almonds and dust with icing sugar. Decorate with the reserved strawberries.

CLEMENTINE CAKE

Preheat the oven to 180°C/350°F/ Gas Mark 4. Grease an 18-cm/ 7-inch round cake tin and base-line with non-stick baking paper.

Pare the rind from the clementines and chop it finely. Cream the butter, sugar and clementine rind together in a bowl until pale and fluffy.

Add the eggs, a little at a time, beating well after each addition. Gently fold in the flour, ground almonds and cream. Spoon the mixture into the prepared tin.

Bake in the preheated oven for 55-60 minutes, or until a fine skewer inserted into the centre comes out clean. Leave to cool slightly.

Meanwhile, to make the glaze, put the clementine juice in a small saucepan with the caster sugar over a medium-low heat. Bring to the boil, then reduce the heat and simmer for 5 minutes.

Turn out the cake onto a wire rack. Drizzle the glaze over the cake until it has been absorbed and sprinkle with the crushed sugar lumps. Leave to cool completely before serving.

SERVES 8

175 g/6 oz butter, softened, plus extra
   for greasing
2 clementines
175 g/6 oz caster sugar
3 eggs, lightly beaten
175 g/6 oz self-raising flour
3 tbsp ground almonds
3 tbsp single cream

GLAZE AND TOPPING

6 tbsp clementine juice
2 tbsp caster sugar
3 white sugar lumps, crushed

This cake is flavoured with clementine rind and juice, creating a rich, buttery cake bursting with fruit flavour. Orange would also work well.

If you prefer, chop the rind from the clementines in a food processor along with the sugar. Tip the mixture into a bowl with the butter and start to cream the mixture.

CARROT CAKE

Preheat the oven to 180°C/350°F/Gas Mark 4. Grease a 20-cm/8-inch square cake tin and line with non-stick baking paper.

Sift the flour, salt and cinnamon into a large bowl and stir in the brown sugar. Add the eggs and oil to the dry ingredients and mix well.

Stir in the carrot, coconut and chopped walnuts.

Pour the mixture into the prepared tin and bake in the preheated oven for 20-25 minutes, or until just firm to the touch. Leave to cool in the tin.

Meanwhile, to make the cream cheese icing, beat the butter, cream cheese, icing sugar and lemon juice together in a bowl until light, fluffy and creamy.

Turn out the cake from the tin. Spread the top with the icing and decorate with a few walnut pieces. Cut into 12 bars or slices.

MAKES 12 BARS/SLICES

butter, for greasing

125 g/4^1/2 oz self-raising flour

pinch of salt

1 tsp ground cinnamon

125 g/4^1/2 oz soft light brown sugar

2 eggs

100 ml/3^1/2 fl oz sunflower oil

175 g/6 oz finely grated carrot

25 g/1 oz grated coconut

2 tbsp chopped walnuts

walnut pieces, to decorate

CREAM CHEESE ICING

4 tbsp butter, softened

55 g/2 oz cream cheese

140 g/5 oz icing sugar, sifted

1 tsp lemon juice

This classic favourite is always popular with children and adults alike when it is served for afternoon tea. It is also good served as a dessert.

For a more moist cake, replace the coconut with a roughly mashed banana.

CRUNCHY FRUIT CAKE

Polenta adds texture to this cake, flavoured with dried fruit and pine kernels, as well as a golden yellow colour. For a more crumbly cake, omit the polenta and use 175 g/6 oz self-raising flour instead.

SERVES 8

125 g/4¹/₂ oz butter, softened, plus
    extra for greasing

115 g/4 oz caster sugar

2 eggs, beaten

55 g/2 oz self-raising flour, sifted

1 tsp baking powder

100 g/3¹/₂ oz polenta

250 g/9 oz mixed dried fruit

25 g/1 oz pine kernels

grated rind of 1 lemon

4 tbsp lemon juice

2 tbsp milk

Preheat the oven to 180°C/350°F/Gas Mark 4. Grease an 18-cm/7-inch round cake tin and base-line with non-stick baking paper.

Cream the butter and sugar together in a bowl until pale and fluffy. Add the eggs, a little at a time, beating well after each addition.

Gently fold the flour, baking powder and polenta into the mixture until well combined.

Gently stir in the dried fruit, pine kernels, grated lemon rind, lemon juice and milk.

Spoon the mixture into the prepared tin and smooth the surface with a knife.

Bake in the preheated oven for 1 hour, or until a skewer inserted into the centre of the cake comes out clean.

Leave the cake to cool in the tin before turning out and serving.

LEMON SYRUP CAKE

Preheat the oven to 180°C/350°F/Gas Mark 4. Grease a 20-cm/8-inch round loose-based cake tin and base-line with non-stick baking paper.

Sift the flour and baking powder together into a bowl and stir in the caster sugar.

Beat the eggs, soured cream, lemon rind and juice and oil together in a separate bowl. Pour the egg mixture into the dry ingredients and mix well until evenly combined.

Pour the mixture into the prepared tin and bake in the preheated oven for 45-60 minutes until risen and golden brown.

Meanwhile, to make the syrup, combine the icing sugar and lemon juice in a small saucepan. Stir over low heat until just starting to bubble and turn syrupy.

As soon as the cake comes out of the oven, prick the surface with a fine skewer, then brush the syrup over the top. Leave the cake to cool completely in the tin before turning out and serving.

SERVES 6-8

butter, for greasing

225 g/8 oz plain flour

2 tsp baking powder

225 g/8 oz caster sugar

4 eggs

150 ml/5 fl oz soured cream

grated rind of 1 large lemon

4 tbsp lemon juice

150 ml/5 fl oz sunflower oil

SYRUP

4 tbsp icing sugar

3 tbsp lemon juice

The lovely light and tangy flavour of the sponge cake is balanced by the lemony syrup poured over the top.

Pricking the surface of the hot cake with a skewer ensures that the syrup seeps right into the cake and the full flavour is absorbed.

MOIST CHOCOLATE CAKE

Preheat the oven to 160°C/325°F/Gas Mark 3. Grease an 850 ml/1¹/2-pint pudding basin. Cream the butter, sugar and vanilla extract together in a bowl until pale and fluffy. Add the eggs, a little at a time, beating well after each addition.

Melt the plain chocolate in a heatproof bowl set over a saucepan of barely simmering water. Gradually stir in the buttermilk until well combined. Remove from the heat and leave to cool slightly.

Sift the flour, bicarbonate of soda and salt together into a separate bowl. Using a metal spoon or spatula, gently fold in the chocolate mixture alternately with the flour mixture into the creamed mixture, a little at a time. Spoon the cake mixture into the prepared pudding basin and smooth the surface.

Bake in the preheated oven for 50 minutes, or until a skewer inserted into the centre of the cake comes out clean. Turn out onto a wire rack and leave to cool.

Meanwhile, to make the icing, put the marshmallows and milk in a small saucepan over a very low heat and heat until the marshmallows have melted. Remove from the heat and leave to cool.

Whisk the egg whites in a large, clean bowl until soft peaks form, then add the sugar and continue whisking until stiff peaks form. Fold the egg white mixture into the cooled marshmallow mixture and set aside for 10 minutes.

When the cake is cool, cover the top and side with the marshmallow icing. Top with grated milk chocolate.

MAKES ONE 15-CM/ 6-INCH CAKE

90 g/3¹/4 oz butter, preferably
   unsalted, plus extra for greasing

225 g/8 oz caster sugar

¹/2 tsp vanilla extract

2 eggs, lightly beaten

85 g/3 oz plain chocolate,
   broken into pieces

5 tbsp buttermilk

175 g/6 oz self-raising flour

¹/2 tsp bicarbonate of soda

pinch of salt

55 g/2 oz milk chocolate, grated,
   to decorate

MARSHMALLOW ICING

175 g/6 oz white marshmallows

1 tbsp milk

2 egg whites

2 tbsp caster sugar

The sweetness of the whipped marshmallow icing complements the mouthwatering flavour of this moist plain chocolate sponge.

GINGERBREAD

This spicy gingerbread is made even more moist and flavourful by the addition of chopped fresh apples. Serve as a mid-afternoon snack. If you enjoy the flavour of ginger, try adding 1 tablespoon finely chopped stem ginger to the mixture.

MAKES 12 BARS

- 175 g/6 oz butter, plus extra for greasing
- 175 g/6 oz soft light brown sugar
- 2 tbsp black treacle
- 225 g/8 oz plain flour
- 1 tsp baking powder
- 2 tsp bicarbonate of soda
- 2 tsp ground ginger
- 150 ml/5 fl oz milk
- 1 egg, lightly beaten
- 2 eating apples, peeled, chopped and tossed in 1 tbsp lemon juice

Preheat the oven to 160°C/325°F/Gas Mark 3. Grease a 23-cm/9-inch square cake tin and line with non-stick baking paper.

Heat the butter, sugar and black treacle in a saucepan over a low heat, stirring, until melted. Remove from the heat and leave to cool.

Sift the flour, baking powder, bicarbonate of soda and ginger together into a large bowl.

Stir in the milk, egg and the butter mixture, followed by the apples tossed in the lemon juice.

Mix together gently, then pour the mixture into the prepared tin.

Bake in the preheated oven for 30-35 minutes until well risen and a skewer inserted into the centre of the cake comes out clean.

Leave the cake to cool in the tin before turning out and cutting into 12 bars.

YOGURT CACHE

SERVES 8

150 ml/5 fl oz sunflower or corn oil,
   plus extra for oiling

150 ml/5 fl oz yogurt, plus extra
   to serve

250 g/9 oz caster sugar

250 g/9 oz self-raising flour

2 eggs

juice and finely grated rind of
   2 large lemons

70 g/2^{1}/$_{2}$ oz white granulated sugar

2 tbsp Greek honey

25 g/1 oz toasted flaked almonds,
   to decorate

YOGURT CAKE

Preheat the oven to 180°C/350°F/Gas Mark 4. Oil a 20-cm/8-inch round loose-based cake tin and line with greaseproof paper.

Put the yogurt, oil, caster sugar, flour, eggs and lemon rind in a large bowl or food processor and beat together or process until smooth.

Turn the mixture into the prepared cake tin and bake in the preheated oven for 1^{1}/$_{4}$ hours, or until golden brown and a skewer inserted into the centre of the cake comes out clean.

Meanwhile, put the lemon juice and granulated sugar in a saucepan over a low heat and heat until the sugar has dissolved. Bring to the boil, then reduce the heat and simmer for 2–3 minutes. Stir in the honey.

When the cake is cooked, carefully turn out and transfer to a wire rack set over a tray. Prick the top of the cake all over with a fine skewer. If necessary, reheat the lemon syrup, then pour the hot syrup over the warm cake and leave to cool. Scatter over the flaked almonds to decorate before serving. Serve with Greek yogurt.

This is a light, moist cake, finished with a tangy lemon and honey syrup.

WALNUT CAKE

SERVES 12

115 g/4 oz butter, softened, plus extra
   for greasing

115 g/4 oz self-raising flour

1/2 tsp ground cinnamon

1/4 tsp ground cloves

115 g/4 oz caster sugar

4 eggs

225 g/8 oz walnut pieces,
   finely chopped

juice and pared rind of 1 orange

115 g/4 oz white granulated sugar

2 tbsp brandy

Preheat the oven to 190°C/375°F/Gas Mark 5. Grease and base-line a deep roasting tin measuring 25 x 18 cm/10 x 7 inches with greaseproof paper.

Sift the flour, cinnamon and cloves together into a bowl. Cream the butter and caster sugar together in a large bowl until pale and fluffy. Add the eggs, one at a time, beating well after each addition. Using a metal spoon or spatula, gently fold in the flour mixture, then fold in the chopped walnuts.

Turn the mixture into the prepared tin and bake in the preheated oven for 30 minutes, or until risen and springy to the touch.

Meanwhile, put the orange juice in a measuring jug and make up to 150 ml/5 fl oz with water. Pour into a saucepan, add the granulated sugar and the pared orange rind and heat over a low heat until the sugar has dissolved. Bring to the boil and boil for 6 minutes until the mixture begins to thicken. Remove from the heat and stir in the brandy.

When the cake is cooked, prick the surface all over with a fine skewer, then strain the hot syrup over the top of the cake. Leave in the tin for at least 4 hours before serving.

This moist walnut cake is made a little more special by being topped with a fragrant orange- and brandy-flavoured syrup.

STRAWBERRY CHEESECAKE

Sweet strawberries are teamed with creamy mascarpone cheese and luxurious white chocolate to make this mouthwatering cheesecake.

SERVES 8

BASE

55 g/2 oz butter, preferably unsalted

200 g/7 oz crushed digestive biscuits

85 g/3 oz chopped walnuts

FILLING

450 g/1 lb mascarpone cheese

2 eggs, beaten

3 tbsp caster sugar

250 g/9 oz white chocolate, broken into pieces

300 g/10^1/$_2$ oz strawberries, hulled and quartered

TOPPING

175 g/6 oz mascarpone cheese

ready-made chocolate caraque

16 whole strawberries

Preheat the oven to 150°C/300°F/Gas Mark 2. Melt the butter in a saucepan over a low heat and stir in the crushed biscuits and nuts. Spoon into a 23-cm/9-inch round springform cake tin and press evenly over the base with the back of a spoon. Set aside.

To make the filling, beat the mascarpone cheese in a bowl until smooth, then beat in the eggs and sugar. Melt the white chocolate in a heatproof bowl set over a saucepan of barely simmering water, stirring until smooth. Remove from the heat and leave to cool slightly, then stir into the cheese mixture. Stir in the strawberries.

Spoon the mixture into the cake tin, spread out evenly and smooth the surface. Bake in the preheated oven for 1 hour, or until the filling is just firm. Turn off the oven and leave the cheesecake to cool inside with the door slightly ajar until completely cold.

Transfer to a serving plate and spread the mascarpone cheese on top. Decorate with chocolate caraque and the whole strawberries.

RICOTTA CHEESECAKE

SERVES 6-8

PASTRY

175 g/6 oz plain flour, plus extra
    for dusting

3 tbsp caster sugar

pinch of salt

115 g/4 oz unsalted butter, diced
    and chilled, plus extra for greasing

1 egg yolk

FILLING

450 g/1 lb ricotta cheese

125 ml/4 fl oz double cream

2 eggs, plus 1 egg yolk

85 g/3 oz caster sugar

finely grated rind of 1 lemon

finely grated rind of 1 orange

Grease a 20-cm/8-inch round loose-based flan tin. To make the pastry, sift the flour, sugar and salt together onto a work surface and make a well in the centre. Add the butter and egg yolk to the well and, using your fingertips, gradually work in the flour mixture until well combined.

Gather up the dough and knead very lightly on a lightly floured work surface. Cut off about one-quarter, wrap in clingfilm and chill in the refrigerator. Press the remaining dough into the base of the flan tin. Chill in the refrigerator for 30 minutes.

To make the filling, beat the ricotta cheese, cream, eggs and egg yolk, sugar and lemon and orange rinds together in a bowl. Cover with clingfilm and chill in the refrigerator until required.

When ready to bake, preheat the oven to 190°C/375°F/Gas Mark 5. Prick the base of the pastry case all over with a fork. Line with foil, fill with baking beans and bake in a preheated oven for 15 minutes.

Remove the foil and beans, transfer the tin to a wire rack and leave to cool.

Spoon the ricotta mixture into the pastry case and smooth the surface. Roll out the reserved pastry on a lightly floured work surface and cut into strips. Arrange the strips over the filling in a lattice pattern, brushing the overlapping ends with a little water so that they stick.

Bake in the oven for 30-35 minutes until the top of the cheesecake is golden and the filling has set. Transfer to a wire rack and leave to cool before carefully removing from the tin. Cut into wedges to serve.

HOT CHOCOLATE CHEESECAKE

Grease a 20-cm/8-inch round loose-based cake tin. To make the pastry, sift the flour and cocoa powder together into a bowl and rub in the butter with your fingertips until the mixture resembles fine breadcrumbs. Stir in the sugar and ground almonds.

Add the egg yolk and sufficient water to form a soft dough.

Roll out the pastry on a lightly floured work surface and use to line the prepared tin. Chill in the refrigerator for 30 minutes.

When ready to bake, preheat the oven to 160°C/325°F/Gas Mark 3. To make the filling, beat the egg yolks and sugar together in a large bowl until thick and pale. Beat in the cream cheese, ground almonds, cream, cocoa powder and vanilla extract until well combined.

Whisk the egg whites in a separate large, clean bowl until stiff but not dry. Stir a little of the egg white into the cheese mixture, then fold in the remainder. Pour into the pastry case. Bake in the oven for 1½ hours, or until well risen and just firm to the touch. Carefully remove from the tin and dust with icing sugar.

Serve the cheesecake warm.

SERVES 8–10

PASTRY

4 tbsp butter, plus extra for greasing

150 g/5½ oz plain flour, plus extra for dusting

2 tbsp cocoa powder

2 tbsp golden caster sugar

25 g/1 oz ground almonds

1 egg yolk

FILLING

2 eggs, separated

75 g/2¾ oz golden caster sugar

350 g/12 oz cream cheese

4 tbsp ground almonds

150 ml/5 fl oz double cream

25 g/1 oz cocoa powder, sifted

1 tsp vanilla extract

icing sugar, for dusting

This rich cheesecake has chocolate in the pastry and in the filling. Your guests are sure to come back for more!

cakes AND tarts FOR *special* occasions

No special occasion is quite complete without the presence of a lavish cake or tart. Desserts such as torte, vacherin and gâteau may require a little more preparation than the average sponge, but they are the perfect ending to a lovingly prepared meal, or a decadent dinner party. The mouthwatering recipes in this chapter will challenge your baking skills, unleash your creative powers, and cause a jaw or two to drop in delight!

LEMON MERINGUE PIE

Grease a 25-cm/10-inch round fluted flan tin. Roll out the pastry on a lightly floured work surface into a round 5 cm/2 inches larger than the flan tin. Ease the pastry into the tin without stretching and press down lightly into the corners. Roll the rolling pin over the tin to neaten and trim the edge. Prick the base of the flan case all over with a fork. Chill in the refrigerator for 20-30 minutes.

When ready to bake, put a baking sheet in the oven and preheat the oven to 200ºC/400ºF/Gas Mark 6. Line the pastry case with baking paper and fill with baking beans. Bake on the hot baking sheet in the preheated oven for 15 minutes. Remove the beans and paper and bake for a further 10 minutes until the pastry is dry and just colouring. Remove from the oven and reduce the temperature to 150ºC/300ºF/Gas Mark 2.

Put the cornflour, caster sugar and lemon rind into a saucepan. Pour in a little of the water and blend to a smooth paste. Gradually add the remaining water and the lemon juice. Bring to the boil over a medium heat, stirring constantly. Reduce the heat and simmer gently for 1 minute until smooth and glossy. Remove from the heat and beat in the egg yolks, one at a time, then beat in the butter. Put the saucepan in a bowl of cold water to cool the filling. When cool, spoon the mixture into the pastry case.

To make the meringue, using a hand-held electric whisk, beat the egg whites in a large, clean bowl until thick and soft peaks form. Gradually add the caster sugar, beating well after each addition – the mixture should be glossy and firm. Spoon the meringue over the filling to cover it completely and make a seal with the pastry case. Swirl the meringue into peaks and sprinkle with the granulated sugar.

Bake in the preheated oven for 20-30 minutes until the meringue is crisp and pale gold (the centre should still be soft). Leave to cool slightly before serving.

SERVES 8-10

55 g/2 oz unsalted butter, diced,
  plus extra for greasing
250 g/9 oz ready-rolled shortcrust
  pastry, thawed if frozen
plain flour, for dusting
3 tbsp cornflour
85 g/3 oz caster sugar
grated rind of 3 lemons
300 ml/10 fl oz cold water
150 ml/5 fl oz lemon juice
3 egg yolks

MERINGUE
3 egg whites
175 g/6 oz caster sugar
1 tsp golden granulated sugar

This pie is a great favourite. As it is a complicated recipe, it is worth making a good-sized one. Try serving warm with some vanilla ice cream.

RICH FRUIT CAKE

Serve this moist, fruit-laden cake for a special occasion. It would also make an excellent Christmas cake.

SERVES 8-10

butter or margarine, for greasing

125 g/4^1/2 oz stoned dates

100 g/3^1/2 oz ready-to-eat dried prunes

200 ml/7 fl oz unsweetened orange juice

2 tbsp black treacle

1 tsp finely grated lemon rind

1 tsp finely grated orange rind

300 g/10^1/2 oz self-raising wholemeal flour

1 tsp ground mixed spice

150 g/5^1/2 oz raisins

150 g/5^1/2 oz sultanas

75 g/2^3/4 oz currants

150 g/5^1/2 oz dried cranberries

3 large eggs, separated

TO DECORATE

1 tbsp apricot jam, softened

icing sugar, for dusting

175 g/6 oz ready-to-roll fondant icing

strips of orange rind

strips of lemon rind

Preheat the oven to 160°C/325°F/Gas Mark 3. Grease and line a deep 20-cm/8-inch round cake tin with greaseproof paper. Chop the dates and prunes and put in a saucepan. Pour over the orange juice and bring to the boil over a medium-low heat. Reduce the heat and simmer for 10 minutes. Remove from the heat and beat the fruit mixture until puréed. Add the treacle and lemon and orange rinds. Leave to cool.

Sift the flour and mixed spice together into a bowl and add the raisins, sultanas, currants and cranberries. When the date and prune mixture is cool, beat in the egg yolks. Whisk the egg whites in a separate large, clean bowl until stiff peaks form. Spoon the fruit mixture into the dry ingredients and mix together. Gently fold in the egg whites.

Transfer the mixture to the prepared tin and bake in the preheated oven for 1^1/2 hours. Leave to cool in the tin.

Turn out the cake from the tin and brush the top with jam. Dust the work surface with icing sugar and roll out the icing thinly. Lay over the cake top and trim the edges. Decorate with the orange and lemon rind.

RASPBERRY VACHERIN

SERVES 10

3 egg whites

175 g/6 oz caster sugar

1 tsp cornflour

25 g/1 oz plain chocolate, grated

FILLING

**175 g/6 oz plain chocolate, plus extra
to decorate, broken into pieces**

450 ml/16 fl oz double cream, whipped

300 g/10¹/2 oz fresh raspberries

Preheat the oven to 140ºC/275ºF/Gas Mark 1. Draw 3 rectangles, measuring 10 x 25 cm/4 x 10 inches, on sheets of non-stick baking paper and put on 2 baking sheets.

Whisk the egg whites in a large, clean bowl until soft peaks form, then gradually whisk in half the sugar and continue whisking until very stiff and glossy.

Gently fold in the remaining sugar, the cornflour and grated chocolate with a metal spoon or a palette knife.

Spoon the meringue mixture into a piping bag fitted with a 1-cm/¹/2-inch plain nozzle and pipe lines across the baking paper rectangles.

Bake in the preheated oven for 1¹/2 hours, changing the position of the baking sheets halfway through. Without opening the oven, turn off the oven and leave the meringues to cool in the oven, then peel off the baking paper.

To make the filling, melt the chocolate in a heatproof bowl set over a saucepan of barely simmering water and spread it over 2 of the meringue layers. Leave to set.

Put a chocolate-coated meringue on a plate and top with about one-third of the cream and raspberries. Gently put the second chocolate-coated meringue on top and spread with half the remaining cream and raspberries. Put the remaining meringue on top and decorate with the remaining cream and raspberries.

Melt a few extra pieces of plain chocolate in a heatproof bowl set over a saucepan of barely simmering water. Drizzle over the top of the vacherin and serve.

127

PEACH MELBA MERINGUE ROULADE

SERVES 8

sunflower oil, for oiling

COULIS
350 g/12 oz fresh raspberries
115 g/4 oz icing sugar

MERINGUE
2 tsp cornflour
300 g/10^1/2 oz caster sugar
5 large egg whites
1 tsp cider vinegar

FILLING
3 peaches, peeled, stoned
   and chopped
250 g/9 oz fresh raspberries
200 ml/7 fl oz crème fraîche
150 ml/5 fl oz double cream

Preheat the oven to 150°C/300°F/Gas Mark 2. Oil a 35 x 25-cm/14 x 10-inch Swiss roll tin and line with non-stick baking paper. To make the coulis, process the raspberries and icing sugar in a food processor or blender to a purée. Press through a nylon sieve. To make the meringue, sift the cornflour into a bowl and stir in the caster sugar. Whisk the egg whites in a separate large, clean bowl until stiff peaks form. Whisk in the vinegar. Gradually whisk in the cornflour mixture until stiff and glossy.

Spread the mixture evenly in the prepared tin, leaving a 1-cm/^{1}/2-inch border along one short edge. Bake in the centre of the preheated oven for 20 minutes, then reduce the heat to 110°C/225°F/Gas Mark ^{1}/4 and bake for a further 25–30 minutes, or until puffed up. Leave to cool for 15 minutes, then turn out onto non-stick baking paper.

To make the filling, mix the peaches, raspberries and 2 tablespoons of the coulis together in a bowl. Whip the crème fraîche and cream together in a separate bowl until thick. Spread over the meringue. Scatter the fruit mixture over the cream, leaving a 3-cm/1^1/4-inch border at one short edge. Using the baking paper, lift and roll the meringue, starting at the short edge without the border, ending up seam-side down. Lift onto a plate and serve with the remaining coulis.

This cloud of meringue is a dessert to die for - crunchy on the outside and gooey within. The meringue can be made up to 8 hours before being filled, and once assembled, the roulade will keep for up to 2 days in the refrigerator.

CHERRY AND CHOCOLATE MERINGUE

SERVES 4

4 large egg whites

200 g/7 oz caster sugar

1 tsp cornflour, sifted

1 tsp white wine vinegar

1 tbsp cocoa powder

140 g/5 oz plain chocolate, chopped

ready-made chocolate caraque, to
   decorate

TOPPING

400 ml/14 fl oz double cream

25 g/1 oz icing sugar, sifted

4 tbsp maple syrup

4 tbsp unsalted butter

450 g/1 lb black cherries

A luscious, sticky chocolate
meringue base smothered in cream
and luscious cherries.

Preheat the oven to 140°C/275°F/Gas Mark 1. Line a baking sheet with non-stick baking paper.

Whisk the egg whites in a large, clean bowl until stiff peaks form. Gradually whisk in the caster sugar and continue whisking until very stiff and glossy. Fold in the cornflour, vinegar, cocoa powder and chocolate. Spread onto the baking sheet to form a 24-cm/9½-inch round. Bake in the preheated oven for 1½ hours.

Turn off the oven and leave the meringue in the oven for 45 minutes.

To make the topping, whisk the cream and icing sugar together in a bowl until stiff. Cover and chill in the refrigerator. Stone most of the cherries, reserving a few whole. Melt the maple syrup with the butter in a frying pan and stir in the stoned cherries to coat. Leave to cool.

When the meringue is cold, peel off the baking paper.

To serve, put the meringue on a dish. Spoon the cream mixture into the centre and pile on the cherries, using the whole ones around the edge. Top with the chocolate caraque.

ICED CHOCOLATE TORTE

Preheat the oven to 180°C/350°F/Gas Mark 4. Grease and base-line a 20-cm/8-inch round springform cake tin. Using a hand-held electric whisk, beat the eggs and caster sugar together in a large bowl until thick and pale – the mixture should leave a trail when the whisk is lifted.

Sift in the flour and fold in gently with a metal spoon or a palette knife. Pour into the prepared tin and bake in the preheated oven for 35–40 minutes, or until springy to the touch. Leave to cool slightly in the tin, then transfer to a wire rack and leave to cool completely.

Meanwhile, to make the chocolate cream, bring the cream to the boil in a saucepan, stirring constantly. Add the plain chocolate and stir until melted and well combined. Remove from the heat, transfer to a bowl and leave to cool. Beat with a wooden spoon until thick.

When the cake is cold, cut horizontally in half. Sandwich the layers together with the chocolate cream. Transfer to a wire rack.

To make the icing, melt the white chocolate and butter together in a heatproof bowl set over a saucepan of barely simmering water, stirring until blended. Whisk in the milk and icing sugar, and continue whisking until cool. Pour the icing over the cake and spread with a palette knife to coat the top and side. Decorate with chocolate caraque and leave the icing to set before serving.

SERVES 6

butter, for greasing

4 eggs

115 g/4 oz caster sugar

115 g/4 oz plain flour

plain chocolate caraque, to decorate

CHOCOLATE CREAM

150 ml/5 fl oz double cream

150 g/5$\frac{1}{2}$ oz continental plain
   chocolate, broken into pieces

ICING

75 g/2^3/4 oz white chocolate, broken
   into pieces

1 tbsp butter

1 tbsp milk

4 tbsp icing sugar, sifted

If you can't decide whether you prefer dark chocolate or rich, creamy white chocolate, then this gâteau is definitely for you.

DEVIL'S FOOD CAKE

Preheat the oven to 190°C/375°F/Gas Mark 5. Grease and base-line 2 x 20-cm/8-inch shallow cake tins. Melt the chocolate in a heatproof bowl set over a saucepan of barely simmering water. Sift the flour and bicarbonate of soda together into a bowl.

Cream the butter and sugar together in a separate bowl until pale and fluffy. Beat in the vanilla extract and the eggs, one at a time, beating well after each addition. Add a little flour if the mixture starts to curdle.

Fold the melted chocolate into the mixture until well blended. Gradually fold in the remaining flour, then stir in the buttermilk and boiling water.

Divide the mixture between the prepared tins and smooth the surfaces. Bake in the preheated oven for 30 minutes, or until springy to the touch. Leave the cakes to cool slightly in the tins, then transfer to a wire rack and leave to cool completely.

Put all the icing ingredients in a large heatproof bowl set over a saucepan of gently simmering water. Using a hand-held electric whisk, beat until thick and soft peaks form. Remove from the heat and beat until cool.

Sandwich the cakes together with some of the icing. Swirl the remainder over the top and side of the cake. Decorate with crystalized orange rind.

SERVES 6

225 g/8 oz butter, plus extra
  for greasing
100 g/3¹/₂ oz plain chocolate, broken
  into pieces
325 g/11¹/₂ oz self-raising flour
1 tsp bicarbonate of soda
500 g/1 lb 2 oz soft light brown sugar
1 tsp vanilla extract
3 eggs
125 ml/4 fl oz buttermilk
200 ml/7 fl oz boiling water
crystalized orange rind, to decorate

ICING
225 g/8 oz caster sugar
2 egg whites
1 tbsp lemon juice
3 tbsp orange juice

This classic melt-in-the-mouth chocolate cake is given a tangy citrus-flavoured icing in this recipe.

CHOCOLATE FUDGE GATEAU

SERVES 10

1 tsp sunflower oil, for oiling

85 g/3 oz plain chocolate

225 g/8 oz butter, softened

225 g/8 oz light muscovado sugar

4 eggs, beaten

225 g/8 oz self-raising flour

55 g/2 oz ground almonds

1–2 tbsp cooled, boiled water

115 g/4 oz soft vanilla fudge, diced

ICING

175 g/6 oz butter, softened

280 g/10 oz icing sugar, sifted

3–4 tbsp single cream

55 g/2 oz light muscovado sugar

1 tbsp cocoa powder, sifted

TO DECORATE

55 g/2 oz plain chocolate, grated

cocoa powder-dusted truffles

Preheat the oven to 180°C/350°F/Gas Mark 4. Lightly oil and base-line 2 x 20-cm/8-inch shallow cake tins with non-stick baking paper. Melt the chocolate in a heatproof bowl set over a saucepan of barely simmering water. Cream the butter and muscovado sugar together in a bowl until light and fluffy, then gradually add the eggs, beating well and adding a little of the flour after each addition. Gently fold in the melted chocolate and then the remaining flour until combined.

Stir in the ground almonds with 1–2 tablespoons of cooled boiled water. Mix to form a soft dropping consistency. Stir in the fudge pieces, then divide between the prepared cake tins and smooth the surfaces.

Bake in the preheated oven for 35–40 minutes, or until springy to the touch. Leave the cakes to cool slightly in the tins, then transfer to a wire rack and leave to cool completely.

To make the icing, beat the butter in a bowl until soft and creamy, then gradually beat in the icing sugar, adding a little of the cream as the mixture becomes stiff. Add the muscovado sugar with the cocoa powder and gently stir. Stir in sufficient of the remaining cream to give a soft, spreadable icing.

Put the grated chocolate on a sheet of non-stick baking paper. Cut the cakes horizontally in half and sandwich together with one-third of the icing. Spread another third around the side, then roll the cake in the grated chocolate. Transfer to a serving plate. Spread the top with the remaining icing, piping rosettes around the outside edge for an attractive finish. Decorate with the truffles before serving the gâteau.

This gâteau is absolutely delicious and combines all of the most wickedly delectable ingredients.

SACHERTORTE

SERVES 10

140 g/5 oz butter, preferably unsalted,
plus extra for greasing

175 g/6 oz continental plain chocolate,
broken into pieces

140 g/5 oz caster sugar

6 eggs, separated

175 g/6 oz plain flour

ICING AND FILLING

225 g/8 oz continental plain
chocolate, broken into pieces

5 tbsp cold strong black coffee

115 g/4 oz icing sugar, sifted

6 tbsp good-quality apricot jam,
warmed

Preheat the oven to 150°C/ 300°F/Gas Mark 2. Grease and base-line a 23-cm/9-inch round springform cake tin. Melt the chocolate in a heatproof bowl set over a saucepan of barely simmering water. Cream the butter and 70 g/2^1/2 oz of the caster sugar in a bowl until pale and fluffy. Add the egg yolks and beat well. Add the melted chocolate in a thin stream, beating well. Sift the flour, then fold into the mixture. Whisk the egg whites in a separate large, clean bowl until soft peaks form. Add the remaining caster sugar and whisk until stiff and glossy. Fold half into the chocolate mixture, then fold in the remainder.

Spoon into the prepared tin and smooth the surface. Bake in the preheated oven for 1–1^1/4 hours, or until a skewer inserted into the centre comes out clean. Leave the cake to cool slightly in the tin, then transfer to a wire rack and leave to cool completely.

To make the icing, melt 175 g/6 oz of the chocolate in a heatproof bowl set over a saucepan of barely simmering water. Beat in the coffee. Whisk into the icing sugar in a bowl to form a thick icing. Cut the cake horizontally in half. Sandwich the layers together with the jam. Invert the cake onto a wire rack. Spoon over the icing and spread to coat the top and side. Leave to set for 5 minutes, letting any excess drip through the rack. Transfer to a serving plate and leave to set for at least 2 hours.

Melt the remaining chocolate and spoon into a piping bag fitted with a fine plain nozzle. Pipe 'Sachertorte' on the cake top and leave to set.

PASSION FRUIT ANGEL CAKE

SERVES 8

90 g/3¼ oz plain flour

280 g/10 oz caster sugar

8 large egg whites

1 tsp cream of tartar

pinch of salt

1 tsp vanilla extract

2 tbsp warm water

ICING

4 passion fruit

175 g/6 oz icing sugar

Angel cake is wonderfully light and airy. A passion fruit icing makes it even more delicious.

If you do not have an angel cake tin, any other tin can be used.

Preheat the oven to 180°C/350°F/Gas Mark 4. Sift the flour and 2 tablespoons of the caster sugar together onto a sheet of greaseproof paper. Put the egg whites in a large, clean bowl and whisk until frothy, then stir in the cream of tartar and salt. Sprinkle in the vanilla extract and warm water and continue whisking until the egg whites are stiff but not dry. Sift in the remaining caster sugar, 2 tablespoons at a time, whisking well after each addition, until soft peaks form.

Gradually fold in the flour mixture gently. Pour the mixture into a non-stick angel cake tin with a funnel – it should be about two-thirds full. Bake in the preheated oven for 50-55 minutes until the top is brown and dry to the touch. Invert the tin and leave until the cake is completely cold. Ease the cake out of the tin with a palette knife and transfer to a serving plate.

To make the icing, halve the passion fruit and scoop out the pulp into a sieve set over a bowl. Press the juice from the pulp with a wooden spoon. Stir in enough icing sugar to make an icing with the consistency of double cream. Pour the icing over the cake and leave to set.

SIMNEL CAKE

Line a 23-cm/9-inch round cake tin with greaseproof paper and grease it thoroughly.

Wash the cherries and pat dry, then halve them. Finely chop the almonds. Mix the dried fruit, peel, nuts and the lemon and orange rinds together in a bowl. Add half the amaretto and leave to stand for 1 hour.

Preheat the oven to 180°C/350°F/Gas Mark 4.

Cream the butter and sugar together in a bowl until pale and fluffy. Add the eggs, a little at a time, beating well after each addition. Using a grater, coarsely grate 115 g/4 oz of the marzipan. Add to the soaked fruit with the creamed mixture. Sift the baking powder, cinnamon and flour together and fold in gently.

SERVES 8-10

225 g/8 oz unsalted butter, plus extra for greasing

115 g/4 oz glacé cherries

55 g/2 oz whole blanched almonds

350 g/12 oz sultanas

350 g/12 oz currants

350 g/12 oz raisins

115 g/4 oz mixed peel

55 g/2 oz ground almonds

grated rind of 1 lemon

grated rind of 1 orange

5 tbsp amaretto

225 g/8 oz soft light brown sugar

6 eggs, beaten

1 kg/2 lb 4 oz ready-made marzipan

1¹/₂ tsp baking powder

1 tsp ground cinnamon

280 g/10 oz plain flour

lightly beaten egg white, for brushing

Put half the mixture in the prepared cake tin and smooth the surface. Roll out half the remaining marzipan into a 20-cm/8-inch round and put into the cake tin. Cover with the remaining cake mixture. Smooth over, making a slight dip in the centre.

Bake in the preheated oven for 1 hour, then reduce the temperature to 160°C/325°F/Gas Mark 3. Bake for a further 2 hours, then test with a skewer inserted into the centre. If the skewer does not come out clean, bake for a further 30-45 minutes.

Transfer the cake to a wire rack. Prick the surface of the cake lightly with a fork or skewer. Pour over the remaining amaretto and leave the cake to cool completely before removing from the tin. Keep the cake covered in greaseproof paper with a layer of foil until required.

Brush the cake surface with a little beaten egg white. Use the remaining marzipan to make decorations, such as flowers and leaves, and add to the cake, with twisted strands around the base of the cake.

This is a traditional festive cake. This version includes amaretto, which intensifies its almond flavour and keeps it very moist.

BLACK FOREST ROULADE

SERVES 8-10

1 tsp sunflower oil, for oiling

175 g/6 oz plain chocolate, broken
  into pieces

2-3 tbsp kirsch or brandy

5 eggs

225 g/8 oz caster sugar

2 tbsp icing sugar, sifted

FILLING AND DECORATION

350 ml/12 fl oz double cream

1 tbsp kirsch or brandy

350 g/12 oz fresh black cherries,
  stoned, or 400 g/14 oz canned
  morello cherries, drained
  and stoned

squares of chocolate, to decorate

Preheat the oven to 190°C/375°F/Gas Mark 5. Oil a 35 x 25-cm/14 x 10-inch Swiss roll tin and line with a sheet of non-stick baking paper.

Melt the chocolate in a heatproof bowl set over a saucepan of barely simmering water. Add the kirsch and heat gently, stirring until the mixture is smooth. Remove the bowl from the saucepan and leave to cool.

Put the eggs and sugar in a large heatproof bowl set over the saucepan of barely simmering water. Using a hand-held electric whisk, whisk together until thick and pale – the mixture should leave a trail when the whisk is lifted. Remove the bowl from the saucepan and whisk in the cooled chocolate.

Spoon into the prepared Swiss roll tin, then tap the tin lightly on the work surface to smooth the surface. Bake in the preheated oven for 20 minutes, or until springy to the touch. Remove from the oven and immediately turn out onto a sheet of non-stick baking paper sprinkled with the icing sugar. Peel off the lining paper and roll up the cake tightly, encasing the baking paper. Wrap in a clean tea towel and leave to cool.

Whip the cream in a bowl until soft peaks form, then stir in the kirsch. Reserve 1-2 tablespoons of the cream. Unroll the cake and spread with the remaining cream to within 5 mm/¼ inch of the edges. Reserve a few of the cherries for decoration and scatter the remainder over the cream. Carefully roll up the cake again and transfer to a serving plate. Decorate the top with small rosettes or small spoonfuls of the reserved cream, the reserved cherries and squares of chocolate.

Do not worry if the roulade cracks when it is rolled up. It has a tendency to do this and it does not detract from the sumptuous taste.

PASSION CAKE

Decorating this moist, rich carrot cake lifts it into the celebration class.

SERVES 10

butter, for greasing

150 ml/5 fl oz sunflower or corn oil

175 g/6 oz golden caster sugar

4 tbsp natural yogurt

3 eggs, plus 1 egg yolk

1 tsp vanilla extract

115 g/4 oz walnut pieces, chopped

175 g/6 oz carrots, grated

1 banana, peeled and mashed

225 g/8 oz plain flour

85 g/3 oz fine oatmeal

1 tsp each of bicarbonate of soda,
   baking powder and ground cinnamon

$^{1}/_{2}$ tsp salt

ICING

125 g/4$^{1}/_{2}$ oz cream cheese

4 tbsp natural yogurt

85 g/3 oz icing sugar

1 tsp grated lemon rind

2 tsp lemon juice

TO DECORATE

primroses

1 egg white, lightly beaten

3 tbsp caster sugar

Preheat the oven to 180°C/350°F/Gas Mark 4. Grease and line a 23-cm/ 9-inch round cake tin. Beat the oil, sugar, yogurt, eggs, egg yolk and vanilla extract together in a bowl. Beat in the nuts, carrot, and banana.

Sift the remaining cake ingredients together and gradually beat into the mixture. Pour into the prepared tin and smooth the surface. Bake in the preheated oven for 1$^{1}/_{2}$ hours, or until firm and a fine skewer inserted into the centre comes out clean. Leave to cool in the tin for 15 minutes, then transfer to a wire rack and leave to cool completely.

To make the icing, beat the cream cheese and yogurt together in a bowl. Sift in the icing sugar and stir in the lemon rind and juice. Spread over the top and side of the cake.

To prepare the decoration, dip the flowers quickly in the beaten egg white, then sprinkle with caster sugar to cover the surface completely. Space well apart on non-stick baking paper. Leave in a warm, dry place for several hours until dry and crisp. Arrange on the cake top.

SUMMER FRUIT TARTLETS

SERVES 12

PASTRY
200 g/7 oz plain flour, plus extra
   for dusting
85 g/3 oz icing sugar
55 g/2 oz ground almonds
115 g/4 oz butter
1 egg yolk
1 tbsp milk

FILLING
225 g/8 oz cream cheese
icing sugar, to taste, plus extra
   for dusting
350 g/12 oz fresh summer fruits, such
   as redcurrants, blueberries,
   raspberries and small strawberries

The fruit in the tarts could be
brushed with warmed redcurrant jelly
to make an attractive glaze.

To make the pastry, sift the flour and icing sugar into a bowl. Stir in the ground almonds. Add the butter and rub in until the mixture resembles breadcrumbs. Add the egg yolk and milk and work in with a palette knife, then mix with your fingers until the dough binds together. Wrap the dough in clingfilm and leave to chill in the refrigerator for 30 minutes.

Preheat the oven to 200°C/400°F/Gas Mark 6. On a floured work surface, roll out the pastry and use it to line 12 deep tartlet or individual brioche tins. Prick the bases. Press a piece of foil into each tartlet, covering the edges, and bake in the preheated oven for 10-15 minutes, or until light golden brown. Remove the foil and bake for a further 2-3 minutes. Transfer to a wire rack to cool.

To make the filling, place the cream cheese and icing sugar in a bowl and mix together. Place a spoonful of filling in each pastry case and arrange the fruit on top. Dust with sifted icing sugar and serve immediately.

143

CHOCOLATE AND RASPBERRY TART

SERVES 6

PASTRY

175 g/6 oz plain flour, plus extra
    for dusting

115 g/4 oz butter, chilled

1 tbsp caster sugar

1 egg yolk

FILLING

450 g/1 lb fresh raspberries

2 tbsp flower honey

125 g/4$^{1}/_{2}$ oz white chocolate

250 g/9 oz mascarpone cheese

150 ml/5 fl oz double cream, whipped

This is a very pretty and light white
chocolate tart, swirled with raspberry
sauce and served with fresh
raspberries. This tart would be equally
delicious made with strawberries
or blueberries.

To make the pastry, sift the flour into a bowl. Grate in the butter, then rub in with your fingertips until the mixture resembles fine breadcrumbs. Stir in the sugar, egg yolk and enough cold water to form a soft dough. Roll out on a lightly floured work surface and use to line a 20-cm/8-inch round flan tin. Prick the base all over with a fork and chill in the refrigerator for 30 minutes.

Preheat the oven to 190°C/375°F/Gas Mark 5. Line the tart case with baking paper, fill with baking beans and bake in the preheated oven for 15 minutes. Reduce the temperature to 180°C/350°F/Gas Mark 4, remove the paper and beans and bake for a further 15–20 minutes. Leave to cool in the tin, then transfer the tart case to a serving plate.

Reserve a handful of raspberries, then press the remainder through a nylon sieve into a small saucepan. Stir in the honey. Bring to the boil and boil until thick, then remove from the heat and leave to cool completely.

Melt the chocolate in a heatproof bowl set over a saucepan of barely simmering water. Leave to cool. Mix with the mascarpone cheese and cream. Swirl in the raspberry sauce to give a marbled effect and spoon into the tart case. Decorate with the remaining raspberries and serve.

CHOCOLATE PARFAIT SANDWICHES

This is a novel way of serving a
creamy white chocolate parfait in a
crisp pastry 'sandwich'.
It is the perfect finale to any
dinner-party meal.

For a more elegant version, drizzle a
little melted plain chocolate over the
sandwiches or sprinkle with a little
sifted icing sugar.

SERVES 4

3 large egg whites

140 g/5 oz caster sugar

140 g/5 oz white chocolate, grated

400 ml/14 fl oz whipping cream,
   whipped

350 g/12 oz ready-rolled puff pastry,
   thawed if frozen

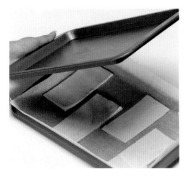

To make the parfait, beat the egg whites and sugar together in a heatproof bowl, then set the bowl over a saucepan of barely simmering water. Using a hand-held electric whisk, beat until stiff peaks form. Remove from the heat, add the chocolate and continue beating until cool. Fold in the cream. Spoon the parfait into a medium, rectangular freezerproof container that allows the parfait a depth of about 5 cm/ 2 inches and freeze for 5-6 hours.

When ready to bake, preheat the oven to 180°C/350°F/Gas Mark 4 and line a baking sheet with non-stick baking paper.

Cut the pastry into 8 regular-sized rectangles large enough to accommodate a slice of the parfait. Transfer the pastry rectangles to the prepared baking sheet and top with another baking sheet, which will keep the pastry flat but crisp. Bake in the preheated oven for 15 minutes. Transfer to a wire rack and leave to cool.

About 20 minutes before you are ready to serve, remove the parfait from the freezer. When it has softened, cut the parfait into slices and put each slice between 2 pieces of pastry to make a 'sandwich'.

HONEY AND LEMON TART

To make the pastry, put the flour, salt, sugar and butter in a food processor. Process in short bursts until the mixture resembles fine breadcrumbs. Sprinkle over the water and mix to form a smooth dough. Alternatively, put the flour, salt and sugar in a bowl and rub in the butter with your fingertips. Add the water and mix to form a smooth dough. For the best results, wrap in foil or clingfilm and chill in the refrigerator for 30 minutes.

Meanwhile, to make the filling, if using cottage cheese, press the cheese through a sieve into a bowl. Add the honey to the cheese and beat until smooth. Add the eggs, cinnamon and lemon rind and juice and mix together well.

When ready to bake, preheat the oven to 200°C/400°F/Gas Mark 6. Roll out the pastry on a lightly floured work surface and use to line a 23-cm/9-inch round fluted flan tin. Transfer to a baking sheet. Line with baking paper and fill with baking beans. Bake in the preheated oven for 15 minutes. Remove the paper and beans and bake for a further 5 minutes, or until the tart base is firm but not browned.

Reduce the oven temperature to 180°C/350°F/Gas Mark 4. Pour the filling into the tart case and bake in the oven for 30 minutes, or until set. Serve cold, decorated with slices of lemon.

SERVES 8-12

PASTRY

225 g/8 oz plain flour, plus extra
   for dusting

pinch of salt

1^1/2 tsp caster sugar

150 g/5^1/2 oz butter, diced
   and chilled

3-4 tbsp iced water

FILLING

375 g/13 oz cottage cheese, cream
   cheese or ricotta cheese

6 tbsp honey

3 eggs, beaten

^{1}/2 tsp ground cinnamon

grated rind and juice of 1 lemon

lemon slices, to decorate

Use a soft, cream cheese for this dessert. Cottage cheese, cream cheese and ricotta are all suitable choices. Choose an aromatic honey such as orange blossom, for a good flavour.

CHOCOLATE CHERRY GATEAU

Chocolate and cherries is a classic combination. This is the perfect cake for all special occasions.

MAKES ONE 23-CM/ 9-INCH CAKE

3 tbsp butter, preferably unsalted, melted, plus extra for greasing

1 kg/2 lb 4 oz fresh cherries, stoned and halved

225 g/8 oz caster sugar

100 ml/3¹/2 fl oz cherry brandy

125 g/4¹/2 oz plain flour

55 g/2 oz cocoa powder

¹/2 tsp baking powder

4 eggs

1 litre/1³/4 pints double cream

TO DECORATE

grated continental plain chocolate

whole fresh cherries

Preheat the oven to 180°C/350°F/Gas Mark 4. Grease and line a 23-cm/ 9-inch round springform cake tin. Put the cherries in a saucepan and add 3 tablespoons of the sugar and the cherry brandy. Simmer for 5 minutes. Sieve and set the syrup and cherries aside separately. Sift the flour, cocoa powder and baking powder together into a separate bowl.

Put the eggs in a heatproof bowl and beat in all but 2 tablespoons of the remaining sugar. Set the bowl over a saucepan of barely simmering water. Using a hand-held electric whisk, beat until thickened. Remove from the heat, then gradually fold in the flour mixture and the melted butter. Spoon into the prepared cake tin and smooth the surface. Bake in the preheated oven for 40 minutes. Leave to cool in the tin.

Turn out the cake and cut horizontally in half. Whip the cream with the remaining sugar until soft peaks form. Spread the syrup over the cut sides of the cake and spread cream on one cut side. Arrange the cherries on the cream and cover with more cream. Cover with the other cake half, syrup side down, then cover the top of the cake with cream. Press grated chocolate over the top and side. Decorate with whole cherries.

MOCHA LAYER CAKE

Preheat the oven to 180°C/350°F/Gas Mark 4. Lightly grease 3 x 18-cm/ 7-inch shallow cake tins.

Sift the flour, baking powder and cocoa powder together into a large bowl. Stir in the caster sugar. Make a well in the centre. Add the eggs, syrup, oil and milk to the well and gradually beat in with a wooden spoon to form a smooth mixture. Divide between the prepared tins.

Bake in the preheated oven for 35–45 minutes, or until springy to the touch. Leave to cool slightly in the tins, then transfer to a wire rack and leave to cool completely.

To make the filling, dissolve the coffee in the boiling water and put in a bowl with the cream and icing sugar. Whip until the cream is just holding its shape. Use half the cream to sandwich the 3 cakes together. Spread the remaining cream over the top and side of the cake. Lightly press the chocolate shavings into the cream around the side of the cake.

Transfer to a serving plate. Lay the chocolate caraque over the top of the cake. Cut a few thin strips of baking paper and arrange on top of the caraque. Dust lightly with icing sugar, then carefully remove the paper.

SERVES 8

butter, for greasing

250 g/9 oz self-raising flour

1/4 tsp baking powder

4 tbsp cocoa powder

115 g/4 oz caster sugar

2 eggs

2 tbsp golden syrup

150 ml/5 fl oz sunflower oil

150 ml/5 fl oz milk

FILLING AND TOPPING

1 tsp instant coffee powder

1 tbsp boiling water

300 ml/10 fl oz double cream

2 tbsp icing sugar

TO DECORATE

50 g/1 3/4 oz chocolate shavings

ready made chocolate caraque

icing sugar, for dusting

A delicious combination of chocolate sponge and a creamy coffee filling.

WHITE TRUFFLE CAKE

SERVES 12

butter, for greasing

50 g/1³/4 oz white chocolate

2 eggs

50 g/1³/4 oz caster sugar

70 g/2¹/2 oz plain flour

TRUFFLE TOPPING

300 ml/10 fl oz double cream

350 g/12 oz white chocolate,
   broken into pieces

250 g/9 oz mascarpone cheese

TO DECORATE

ready-made chocolate caraque

cocoa powder, for dusting

Preheat the oven to 180°C/ 350°F/Gas Mark 4. Grease and base-line a 20-cm/8-inch round springform cake tin. Melt the white chocolate in a heatproof bowl set over a saucepan of barely simmering water.

Using a hand-held electric whisk, beat the eggs and sugar together in a large bowl until thick and pale - the mixture should leave a trail when the whisk is lifted. Sift the flour and gently fold into the eggs with a metal spoon or palette knife. Add the melted chocolate. Pour the mixture into the prepared tin and bake in the preheated oven for 25 minutes, or until springy to the touch. Leave to cool slightly in the tin, then transfer to a wire rack and leave to cool completely. Return the cold cake to the tin.

To make the topping, put the cream in a saucepan and bring to the boil, stirring constantly. Leave to cool slightly, then add the white chocolate and stir until melted and combined. Remove from the heat and set aside until almost cool, stirring, then mix in the mascarpone cheese. Pour on top of the cake. Chill in the refrigerator for 2 hours.

To decorate, pick up the caraque carefully and arrange on the top of the dessert, before dusting with cocoa powder.

A light white sponge, topped with a rich creamy-white chocolate truffle mixture, makes an out-of-this-world treat.

scones, teabreads AND muffins

In an age when technology moves at a staggering rate, what could be more reassuringly old-fashioned than tucking into a scone, muffin, or slab of teabread, just like grandmother would have made? Whether it is a summertime scone spread with jam and cream, or a fireside crumpet slathered with butter, there is a heart-warming recipe here for every palate, sweet and savoury.

SCONES

Preheat the oven to 220°C/425°F/Gas Mark 7. Grease a baking sheet.

Sift the flour, salt and baking powder together into a bowl. Rub in the butter with your fingertips until the mixture resembles fine breadcrumbs. Stir in the sugar. Make a well in the centre and pour in the milk. Quickly mix with a round-bladed knife to form a soft dough.

Turn out the dough onto a lightly floured work surface and knead lightly. Roll out to a thickness of about 1 cm/½ inch. Don't be heavy-handed – scones need a light touch. Using a plain 6-cm/2½-inch biscuit cutter, cut out 10-12 rounds and transfer to the prepared baking sheet.

Brush with the milk to glaze and bake in the preheated oven for 10-12 minutes until well risen and golden.

Transfer to a wire rack and leave to cool. Split and serve with clotted cream and strawberry jam.

MAKES 10-12

55 g/2 oz butter, diced and chilled, plus extra for greasing

450 g/1 lb plain flour, plus extra for dusting

½ tsp salt

2 tsp baking powder

2 tbsp caster sugar

250 ml/9 fl oz milk, plus 3 tbsp for glazing

TO SERVE

clotted cream

strawberry jam

Scones are quick to make and are delicious served freshly baked. Scones can be made with or without fruit. Savoury scones, made with a little grated cheese, are also popular and can be served with various fillings as a good alternative to sandwiches.

To make Fruit Scones, add 55 g/2 oz mixed dried fruit with the sugar. To make Wholemeal Scones, use wholemeal flour and omit the sugar. To make Cheese Scones, omit the sugar and fruit and add 55 g/2 oz finely grated Cheddar or Double Gloucester cheese to the mixture with 1 teaspoon mustard.

BUTTERMILK SCONES

Buttermilk makes these scones extra light, and gives them a tangy flavour. Serve with whipped cream and strawberry jam.

MAKES 8

4 tbsp butter, diced and chilled, plus extra for greasing

300 g/10¹/₂ oz self-raising flour, plus extra for dusting

1 tsp baking powder

pinch of salt

40 g/1¹/₂ oz golden caster sugar

300 ml/10 fl oz buttermilk

2 tbsp milk, for glazing

TO SERVE

whipped cream

strawberry jam

Preheat the oven to 220°C/425°F/Gas Mark 7. Grease a baking sheet.

Sift the flour, baking powder and salt together into a bowl. Rub in the butter with your fingertips until the mixture resembles fine breadcrumbs. Stir in the sugar. Make a well in the centre and pour in the buttermilk. Quickly mix with a round-bladed knife to form a soft dough.

Turn out the dough onto a lightly floured work surface and knead lightly. Roll out to a thickness of 2.5 cm/1 inch. Don't be heavy-handed – scones need a light touch. Using a 6-cm/2¹/₂-inch plain or fluted biscuit cutter, cut out 8 rounds and transfer to the prepared baking sheet.

Brush with the milk to glaze and bake in the preheated oven for 12–15 minutes until well risen and golden.

Transfer to a wire rack and leave to cool. Split and serve with whipped cream and strawberry jam.

CHERRY SCONES

Preheat the oven to 220°C/425°F/Gas Mark 7. Grease a baking sheet.

Sift the flour and salt together into a bowl. Rub in the butter with your fingertips until the mixture resembles fine breadcrumbs. Stir in the sugar, cherries and sultanas, then add the beaten egg.

Reserve 1 tablespoon of the milk for glazing. Add the remainder to the mixture. Quickly mix with a round-bladed knife to form a soft dough.

Turn out the dough onto a lightly floured work surface and knead lightly. Roll out to a thickness of 2 cm/3/4 inch. Don't be heavy-handed when rolling the dough – scones need a light touch. Using a 5-cm/2-inch plain or fluted biscuit cutter, cut out 8 rounds and transfer to the prepared baking sheet.

Brush with the remaining milk to glaze and bake in the preheated oven for 8–10 minutes until well risen and golden.

Transfer to a wire rack and leave to cool. Split, spread generously with butter and serve.

MAKES 8

85 g/3 oz butter, diced and chilled,
   plus extra for greasing

225 g/8 oz self-raising flour,
   plus extra for dusting

pinch of salt

1 tbsp caster sugar

3 tbsp glacé cherries, chopped

3 tbsp sultanas

1 egg, lightly beaten

3 tbsp milk

butter, to serve

These are an alternative to traditional scones, using sweet glacé cherries, which not only create colour but add a distinctive flavour. These scones will freeze very successfully, but they are best thawed and eaten within 1 month.

CRUMPETS

MAKES 10-12

350 g/12 oz plain flour

pinch of salt

15 g/^{1}/$_2$ oz fresh yeast

1 tsp caster sugar

400 ml/14 fl oz tepid milk

butter, for greasing and to serve

Sift the flour and salt together into a bowl. Blend the fresh yeast with the sugar in a small bowl and stir in the milk. Make a well in the flour, pour in the yeast mixture and gradually beat in to form a batter. Continue beating until the batter is light and airy. Cover and leave to rise in a warm place for 1 hour, or until well risen.

Stir the batter to knock out any air and check the consistency. If it is too thick, add 1 tablespoon water (it should look rather gloopy). Leave to stand for 10 minutes.

Grease a large frying pan and 4 crumpet rings or 7.5-cm/3-inch plain biscuit cutters. Heat the frying pan over a medium heat for 2 minutes. Arrange the rings in the frying pan and spoon in enough batter to come halfway up each ring. Cook over a low heat for 5-6 minutes until small holes begin to appear and the top is starting to dry.

Remove the crumpet rings with a palette knife or an oven glove. Turn the crumpets over (the base should be golden brown) and cook for 1-2 minutes until cooked through.

Remove the crumpets with a fish slice and keep warm while you cook the remaining batter.

Serve freshly cooked with butter, or if you want to serve them later, leave to cool and reheat in a toaster or by the fire.

Crumpets have always been associated with winter firesides and tea time, and there is nothing nicer than to sit by a roaring fire with a toasting fork in your hand toasting crumpets. Spreading them with lots of butter until it drips through your fingers is also part of enjoying crumpets. Crumpets are now readily available, but to make them at home is a magical experience as the traditional 'bubble' appearance develops.

FUDGE NUT MUFFINS

Chewy pieces of fudge give these muffins a lovely texture and contrast with the crunchiness of the nuts. Store in airtight containers.

MAKES 12

250 g/9 oz plain flour

4 tsp baking powder

85 g/3 oz caster sugar

6 tbsp crunchy
peanut butter

1 egg, beaten

55 g/2 oz butter, melted

175 ml/6 fl oz milk

150 g/5¹/2 oz vanilla fudge, diced

3 tbsp roughly chopped
unsalted peanuts

Preheat the oven to 200°C/400°F/Gas Mark 6. Line a 12-hole muffin tin with muffin paper cases. Sift the flour and baking powder together into a bowl. Stir in the sugar. Add the peanut butter and mix until the mixture resembles breadcrumbs.

Put the egg, butter and milk in a separate bowl and beat together until blended. Stir into the flour mixture until just blended. Lightly stir in the fudge pieces. Do not over-stir the mixture – it is fine for it to be a little lumpy.

Spoon the mixture evenly into the paper cases. Sprinkle the peanuts on top and bake in the preheated oven for 20–25 minutes until well risen and springy to the touch.

Leave the muffins to cool slightly in the tin, then serve, or transfer to a wire rack and leave to cool completely.

DOUBLE CHOCOLATE MUFFINS

MAKES 12

200 g/7 oz plain flour

25 g/1 oz cocoa powder,
   plus extra for dusting

1 tbsp baking powder

1 tsp ground cinnamon

115 g/4 oz golden caster sugar

185 g/6^1/2 oz white chocolate,
   broken into pieces

2 eggs

100 ml/3^1/2 fl oz sunflower oil

225 ml/8 fl oz milk

Chocolate-flavoured muffins with a
white chocolate icing are sure to
please children and adults alike.

When stirring the muffin mixture
together, do not over-stir, otherwise
the muffins will be tough. The mixture
should be quite lumpy.

Preheat the oven to 200°C/400°F/Gas Mark 6. Line a 12-hole muffin tin with muffin paper cases. Sift the flour, cocoa powder, baking powder and cinnamon together into a large bowl. Stir in the sugar and 125 g/4^1/2 oz of the chocolate.

Put the eggs and oil in a separate bowl and whisk together until frothy, then gradually whisk in the milk. Stir into the flour mixture until just blended. Spoon the mixture evenly into the paper cases, filling each three-quarters full.

Bake in the preheated oven for 20 minutes, or until well risen and springy to the touch. Leave the muffins to cool slightly in the tin, then transfer to a wire rack and leave to cool completely.

Melt the remaining chocolate in a heatproof bowl set over a saucepan of barely simmering water and spread over the tops of the muffins. Leave to set, then dust the tops with a little cocoa powder and serve.

APPLE AND CINNAMON MUFFINS

These spicy muffins are quick and easy to make with a few stock ingredients and two apples. The crunchy sugar topping turns them into a real treat.

MAKES 6

90 g/3^1/4 oz plain wholemeal flour

70 g/2^1/2 oz plain white flour

1^1/2 tsp baking powder

pinch of salt

1 tsp ground cinnamon

50 g/1^3/4 oz golden caster sugar

2 small eating apples, peeled, cored and finely chopped

125 ml/4 fl oz milk

1 egg, beaten

55 g/2 oz butter, melted

TOPPING

12 brown sugar cubes, roughly crushed

^{1}/2 tsp ground cinnamon

Preheat the oven to 200°C/400°F/Gas Mark 6. Line 6 holes of a muffin tin with muffin paper cases.

Sift the flours, baking powder, salt and cinnamon together into a large bowl, then stir in the sugar and apples. Put the milk, egg and butter in a separate bowl and beat together until blended. Stir into the flour mixture until just blended. Do not over-stir the mixture – it is fine for it to be a little lumpy.

Spoon the mixture evenly into the paper cases. To make the topping, mix the crushed sugar cubes and cinnamon together and sprinkle over the tops of the muffins. Bake in the preheated oven for 20-25 minutes until well risen and springy to the touch. Leave the muffins to cool slightly in the tin, then serve, or transfer to a wire rack and leave to cool.

Work quickly once you have chopped the apple, as the flesh soon starts to brown on exposure to the air.

BLUEBERRY MUFFINS

MAKES 12

225 g/8 oz plain flour

1 tsp bicarbonate of soda

¼ tsp salt

1 tsp ground mixed spice

115 g/4 oz caster sugar

3 egg whites

3 tbsp margarine

150 ml/5 fl oz thick natural or
   blueberry-flavoured yogurt

1 tsp vanilla extract

115 g/4 oz fresh blueberries

Preheat the oven to 190°C/375°F/Gas Mark 5. Line a 12-hole muffin tin with 12 muffin paper cases. Sift the flour, bicarbonate of soda, salt and half the mixed spice together into a large bowl. Add 6 tablespoons of the sugar and mix together well.

Lightly whisk the egg whites together with a fork in a separate bowl. Add the margarine, yogurt and vanilla extract and beat together until blended, then stir in the blueberries until thoroughly mixed. Stir into the flour mixture until just blended. Do not over-stir the mixture - it is fine for it to be a little lumpy.

Spoon the mixture evenly into the paper cases, filling each about two-thirds full.

Mix the remaining sugar with the remaining mixed spice, then sprinkle over the tops of the muffins. Bake in the preheated oven for 25 minutes, or until well risen and springy to the touch.

Leave the muffins to cool slightly in the tin, then serve, or transfer to a wire rack and leave to cool completely.

Another way to test that your muffins are cooked is to insert a cocktail stick into the centre of one of the muffins. If it comes out clean, they are cooked. If not, return the muffins to the oven and bake for a little longer.

ITALIAN TOMATO MUFFINS

Peel the tomatoes (see below), halve, then scoop out the seeds with a teaspoon and discard. Chop the tomatoes finely and set aside.

Preheat the oven to 200°C/400°F/Gas Mark 6. Lightly oil a 12-hole muffin tin or line with 12 muffin paper cases. Sift the flour, baking powder and salt together into a large bowl. Add the polenta and mix together well.

Lightly whisk the egg and milk together with a fork in a separate bowl. Add the tomatoes, then the garlic, basil and parsley and mix together well. Stir into the flour mixture until just blended. Do not over-stir the mixture – it is fine for it to be a little lumpy.

Spoon the muffin mixture evenly into the muffin holes or the paper cases, filling each about two-thirds full.

Bake in the preheated oven for 20 minutes, or until well risen and springy to the touch.

Leave the muffins to cool slightly in the tin, then serve, or transfer to a wire rack and leave to cool completely.

MAKES 12

300 g/10^1/$_2$ oz Italian plum tomatoes

oil, for oiling (optional)

140 g/5 oz plain flour

2 tbsp baking powder

^{1}/$_2$ tsp salt

200 g/7 oz fine polenta

1 egg, lightly beaten

300 ml/10 fl oz milk

1 garlic clove, crushed

1 tbsp chopped fresh basil

1^1/$_2$ tsp chopped fresh parsley

To peel tomatoes, bring a kettle of water to the boil. Put the tomatoes in a heatproof bowl, then pour over enough boiling water to cover. Leave to soak for about 3 minutes, then remove with a slotted spoon and leave to cool slightly. When the tomatoes are cool enough to handle, gently pierce the skins with the point of a knife. Remove and discard the skins.

CHEESE MUFFINS

MAKES 10

115 g/4 oz self-raising flour

1 tbsp baking powder

1 tsp salt

225 g/8 oz fine polenta

150 g/5^1/2 oz grated mature
   Cheddar cheese

55 g/2 oz butter, melted

2 eggs, beaten

1 garlic clove, crushed

300 ml/10 fl oz milk

Preheat the oven to 200°C/400°F/Gas Mark 6. Line 10 holes of a 12-hole muffin tin with muffin paper cases. Sift the flour, baking powder and salt together into a bowl. Stir in the polenta and 115 g/4 oz of the cheese.

Put the butter, eggs, garlic and milk in a separate bowl and mix together well. Stir into the flour mixture until just blended. Do not over-stir the mixture – it is fine for it to be a little lumpy.

Spoon the mixture evenly into the paper cases, sprinkle over the remaining cheese and bake in the preheated oven for 20-25 minutes until well risen and springy to the touch. Leave the muffins to cool slightly in the tin, then serve, or transfer to a wire rack and leave to cool.

Polenta, or cornmeal, used to be difficult to find, but it is now widely available in most major supermarkets and health-food shops.

SAVOURY LEEK AND HAM MUFFINS

Cooked bacon works as well as ham in these muffins. You can also replace some or all of the Cheddar cheese with a smoked cheese, such as Applewood, for an added smoky flavour.

MAKES 12

2 tbsp vegetable oil

1 leek, trimmed and
    finely chopped

280 g/10 oz plain flour

2 tsp baking powder

$1/2$ tsp bicarbonate of soda

1 egg, lightly beaten

300 ml/10 fl oz thick Greek-style
    natural yogurt

55 g/2 oz butter, melted

25 g/1 oz Cheddar cheese, grated

25 g/1 oz fresh chives, finely snipped

150 g/$5^1/2$ oz cooked ham, chopped

Preheat the oven to 200°C/400°F/Gas Mark 6. Line a 12-hole muffin tin with 12 muffin paper cases.

Heat the oil in a frying pan over a low heat. Add the leek and cook, stirring, for 2 minutes or until the leeks are soft. Remove from the heat and leave to cool.

Sift the flour, baking powder and bicarbonate of soda together into a large bowl. Lightly mix the egg, yogurt and butter together in a separate bowl. Add the cheese, chives, leek and half the chopped ham and mix together well. Stir into the flour mixture until just blended. Do not over-stir the mixture – it is fine for it to be a little lumpy.

Spoon the muffin mixture evenly into the muffin holes or the paper cases, filling each about two-thirds full. Sprinkle over the remaining chopped ham.

Bake in the preheated oven for 20 minutes, or until well risen and springy to the touch. Leave the muffins to cool slightly in the tin, then serve, or transfer to a wire rack and leave to cool completely.

SOURED CREAM MUFFINS WITH CHIVES

MAKES 12

280 g/10 oz plain flour

2 tsp baking powder

$^1/2$ tsp bicarbonate of soda

25 g/1 oz Cheddar cheese, grated

35 g/1$^1/4$ oz fresh chives, finely
   snipped, plus extra to garnish

1 egg, lightly beaten

200 ml/7 fl oz soured cream

100 ml/3$^1/2$ fl oz natural yogurt

55 g/2 oz butter, melted

Preheat the oven to 200°C/400°F/Gas Mark 6. Line a 12-hole muffin tin with 12 muffin paper cases.

Sift the flour, baking powder and bicarbonate of soda together into a large bowl. Add the cheese and chives and mix together well. Lightly mix the egg, soured cream, yogurt and butter together in a separate bowl. Stir into the flour mixture until just blended. Do not over-stir the mixture – it is fine for it to be a little lumpy.

Spoon the muffin mixture evenly into the muffin holes or the paper cases, filling each about two-thirds full. Sprinkle over some extra chives to garnish.

Bake in the preheated oven for 20 minutes, or until well risen and springy to the touch. Leave the muffins to cool slightly in the tin, then serve, or transfer to a wire rack and leave to cool completely.

These muffins are deliciously creamy and a real treat for any picnic, buffet or lunch box. For extra flavour, try stirring 2 tablespoons finely chopped spring onion into the mixture when you add the chives.

WELSH BARA BRITH

Teabreads such as Welsh Bara Brith are traditionally made using yeast and flavoured with fruits and spices. Today, some teabreads are made not with yeast but using bicarbonate of soda or baking powder as a raising agent, but the original recipe using yeast is the best. Serve in thin slices spread with butter.

MAKES 1 LOAF

butter, for greasing

175 ml/6 fl oz milk

4 tsp easy-blend dried yeast

115 g/4 oz soft light brown sugar

450 g/1 lb strong white bread flour,
   plus extra for dusting

1/2 tsp salt

115 g/4 oz butter

280 g/10 oz mixed dried fruit, such as
   sultanas, currants and raisins

55 g/2 oz mixed peel

1 tsp ground mixed spice

1 egg, beaten

Grease a 900-g/2-lb loaf tin.

Warm the milk in a saucepan until tepid and add the yeast with 1 teaspoon of the sugar. Mix well and leave in a warm place for 15 minutes until frothy.

Sift the flour and salt together into a bowl. Rub in the butter with your fingertips until the mixture resembles fine breadcrumbs. Stir in the remaining sugar, dried fruit, mixed peel and mixed spice. Add the egg and the yeast mixture and mix to form a soft dough.

Turn out the dough onto a lightly floured work surface and knead for 5-10 minutes, or until smooth and elastic. Return the dough to the bowl, cover with clingfilm and leave to rise in a warm place for 1-1 1/2 hours until doubled in size. Preheat the oven to 190ºC/375ºF/Gas Mark 5.

Turn out the dough again and knead lightly. Shape into a rectangle the length of the tin and 3 times the width. Fold the dough lengthways into 3 and put in the tin with the join underneath. Cover and leave to prove in a warm place for 30-40 minutes until it has risen above the tin.

Bake towards the bottom of the preheated oven for 30 minutes. Turn the loaf around and cover the top with foil if it is getting too brown. Bake for a further 30 minutes, or until the loaf sounds hollow when tapped on the base.

Transfer to a wire rack and leave to cool completely. Cut into slices and serve.

STICKY GINGER MARMALADE LOAF

Preheat the oven to 180°C/350°F/Gas Mark 4. Grease and line a 900-g/ 2-lb loaf tin.

Put 1 tablespoon of the marmalade in a small saucepan and set aside. Put the remaining marmalade in a bowl with the butter, sugar and eggs. Sift in the flour, baking powder and ginger and beat together until smooth. Stir in three-quarters of the nuts.

Spoon the mixture into the prepared tin and smooth the surface. Sprinkle with the remaining nuts. Bake in the preheated oven for 1 hour, or until well risen and a skewer inserted into the centre comes out clean.

Leave in the tin for 10 minutes, then transfer to a wire rack and leave to cool. Warm the reserved marmalade over a low heat, then brush over the warm loaf. Cut into slices and serve.

MAKES 1 LOAF

175 g/6 oz butter, softened, plus extra
   for greasing
125 g/4^1/2 oz ginger marmalade
175 g/6 oz light muscovado sugar
3 eggs, beaten
225 g/8 oz self-raising flour
^{1}/2 tsp baking powder
1 tsp ground ginger
100 g/3^1/2 oz pecan nuts,
   roughly chopped

Ginger marmalade gives a wonderful flavour to this moist, sticky teabread, which is very quick to prepare.

BANANA AND CHOCOLATE TEABREAD

This is a good loaf to make when you have some over-ripe bananas in the fruit bowl. It will need to be eaten quickly.

MAKES 1 LOAF

115 g/4 oz butter, softened, plus extra
   for greasing

2 ripe bananas, peeled and mashed

85 g/3 oz golden caster sugar

2 eggs

200 g/7 oz self-raising flour

25 g/1 oz cocoa powder

1 tsp baking powder

2 tbsp milk

100 g/3^1/2 oz plain chocolate chips

Preheat the oven to 180°C/350°F/Gas Mark 4. Grease and line a 900-g/ 2-lb loaf tin.

Mix the bananas, butter, sugar and eggs together in a bowl. Sift in the flour, cocoa powder and baking powder. Beat until smooth, adding enough milk to give a thick dropping consistency. Stir in the chocolate chips.

Spoon the mixture into the prepared tin and smooth the surface. Bake in the preheated oven for 50-60 minutes until well risen and a skewer inserted into the centre comes out clean. Leave in the tin for 5 minutes, then transfer to a wire rack and leave to cool completely. Serve in slices, with or without butter.

You can mix the ingredients in a food processor, then stir in the chocolate chips by hand.

CHOCOLATE ORANGE TEABREAD

MAKES 2 LOAVES, EACH SERVING 6

150 g/5^1/2 oz butter, softened, plus
    extra for greasing

75 g/2^3/4 oz plain chocolate,
    broken into pieces

250 g/9 oz golden caster sugar

5 large eggs, beaten

150 g/5^1/2 oz plain flour

2 tsp baking powder

pinch of salt

grated rind of 2 oranges

Preheat the oven to 180°C/350°F/Gas Mark 4. Grease and line 2 x 450-g/1-lb loaf tins.

Melt the chocolate in a large heatproof bowl set over a saucepan of barely simmering water. Remove from the heat.

Cream the butter and sugar together in a separate bowl until light and fluffy. Gradually add the eggs, a little at a time, beating well after each addition. Sift the flour, baking powder and salt together and gently fold into the creamed mixture. Transfer one-third of the mixture to the melted chocolate and stir together. Stir the orange rind into the remaining mixture. Divide half the orange mixture between the prepared loaf tins and spread each into an even layer.

Drop tablespoonfuls of the chocolate mixture on top, dividing it between the 2 tins, but do not spread out. Add the remaining orange mixture to the 2 tins. Using a knife, gently swirl the 2 mixtures together to give a marbled effect. Bake in the preheated oven for 35–40 minutes until a skewer inserted into the centre of each loaf comes out clean. Leave the loaves to cool in the tins for 10 minutes, then transfer to a wire rack and leave to cool completely.

This recipe makes two delicious chocolate-marbled loaves – one to eat now and one to freeze for another day.

DATE AND HONEY LOAF

This bread is full of good things - chopped dates, sesame seeds and honey. Toast thick slices and spread with cream cheese for a light snack.

MAKES 1 LOAF

butter, for greasing

250 g/9 oz strong white bread flour, plus extra for dusting

70 g/2$^{1}/_{2}$ oz strong wholemeal bread flour

$^{1}/_{2}$ tsp salt

1 $^{1}/_{2}$ tsp easy-blend dried yeast

200 ml/7 fl oz tepid water

3 tbsp sunflower oil

3 tbsp honey

85 g/3 oz stoned dates, chopped

2 tbsp sesame seeds

butter or cream cheese, to serve

Grease a 900-g/2-lb loaf tin.

Sift the flours and salt together into a large bowl, then stir in the yeast. Make a well in the centre. Add the water, oil and honey to the well and mix to form a dough.

Turn out the dough on a lightly floured work surface and knead for 5-10 minutes, or until smooth and elastic.

Transfer the dough to a greased bowl, cover and leave to rise in a warm place for 1 hour, or until doubled in size.

Turn out the dough again and knead in the dates and sesame seeds. Shape the dough and put in the prepared tin. Cover and leave to prove in a warm place for 30 minutes, or until springy to the touch. Preheat the oven to 220°C/425°F/Gas Mark 7.

Bake the loaf in the preheated oven for 30 minutes, or until it sounds hollow when tapped on the base.

Transfer the loaf to a wire rack and leave to cool completely. Serve cut into thick slices with butter or cream cheese.

TEACAKES

Grease 2 baking sheets.

Warm the milk in a saucepan until just tepid and add the yeast with 1 teaspoon of the sugar. Mix well and leave in a warm place for 15 minutes until frothy.

Sift the flour, salt and mixed spice together into a large bowl. Stir in the currants, mixed peel and the remaining sugar. Make a well in the centre. Add the yeast mixture, butter and egg to the well and mix using a wooden spoon at first and then by hand to form a dough.

Turn out the dough onto a lightly floured work surface and knead for 5-10 minutes, or until smooth and elastic.

Return the dough to the bowl, cover with clingfilm and leave to rise in a warm place for 40-45 minutes, or until doubled in size.

Turn out the dough again and knead lightly. Cut into 10-12 equal pieces and shape each piece into a bun.

Transfer the buns to the prepared baking sheets, cover with clean, damp tea towels or large polythene bags and leave to prove in a warm place for 30-40 minutes. Preheat the oven to 220ºC/425ºF/Gas Mark 7.

Bake in the preheated oven for 18-20 minutes until golden brown. Transfer to a wire rack and brush with the sugar glaze while still hot.

MAKES 10-12

55 g/2 oz butter, melted, plus extra
    for greasing
300 ml/10 fl oz milk
4 tsp easy-blend dried yeast
55 g/2 oz caster sugar
450 g/1 lb strong white bread flour,
    plus extra for dusting
1 tsp salt
1 tsp ground mixed spice
115 g/4 oz currants
25 g/1 oz mixed candied peel, chopped
1 egg, beaten
sugar glaze made from 2 tbsp sugar
    blended with 2 tbsp warm milk

Teacakes are the basis of a traditional English tea. Afternoon tea was reputed to have been started by the Duchess of Bedford. Teacakes are usually halved, toasted and then served with butter and jam.

sweet yeast breads AND buns

Whether creating a true French-style breakfast, or a high tea spread, sweet yeast breads or buns deserve a place at the table. From Pain aux Chocolat to Brioche, Cinnamon Swirls to Chocolate Bread, this category contains a diverse range of baked delights with a rich variety of textures. Here, sticky buns – such as that old classic, the Chelsea – rub shoulders with doughy snacks like Churros, and fruity breads such as Tropical Fruit Bread with Crown Loaf. As if that were not enough to keep you kneading, there is even a recipe for the German classic Stollen – a more unusual take on the traditional sweet yeast bread.

ORANGE AND CURRANT BRIOCHES

Grease 12 individual brioche moulds. Sift the flour and salt together into a warmed bowl. Stir in the yeast, sugar, raisins and orange rind. Make a well in the centre. Mix the water, eggs and butter together and add to the well. Mix to form a soft dough.

Turn out the dough onto a lightly floured work surface and knead for 5-10 minutes, or until smooth and elastic. Put the dough in an oiled bowl, cover with clingfilm and leave to rise in a warm place for 1 hour, or until doubled in size.

Turn out the dough again, knead lightly for 1 minute, then roll into a sausage shape. Cut into 12 equal pieces. Shape three-quarters of each piece into a ball and transfer to the prepared moulds. With a floured finger, press an indentation in the centre of each. Shape the remaining pieces of dough into little plugs and press one into each indentation.

Put the moulds on a baking sheet, cover lightly with oiled clingfilm and leave in a warm place until the dough comes almost to the top of the moulds. Preheat the oven to 220°C/425°F/Gas Mark 7.

Brush the brioches with beaten egg. Bake in the preheated oven for 15 minutes, or until golden brown. Serve warm with butter.

MAKES 12

55 g/2 oz butter, melted, plus extra
    for greasing and to serve

225 g/8 oz strong white bread flour,
    plus extra for dusting

$^{1}/_{2}$ tsp salt

$1^{1}/_{2}$ tsp easy-blend dried yeast

1 tbsp golden caster sugar

55 g/2 oz raisins

grated rind of 1 orange

2 tbsp tepid water

2 eggs, beaten

oil, for oiling

beaten egg, for glazing

Brioche is a light, rich French bread that can be made as one large loaf
or small buns. They are usually served with coffee for breakfast.
If you do not have brioche moulds, use a muffin tin instead.

BREAKFAST BRIOCHE

SERVES 6-8

oil, for oiling

225 g/8 oz strong white bread flour,
   plus extra for dusting

1/2 tsp salt

1 1/2 tsp easy-blend dried yeast

1 tbsp caster sugar

2 eggs, lightly beaten

2 tbsp tepid milk

55 g/2 oz butter, melted

GLAZE

1 egg yolk

1 tbsp milk or water

Oil a standard-sized brioche mould.

Sift the flour and salt together into a warmed bowl. Sir in the yeast and sugar. Make a well in the centre. Mix the eggs, milk and butter together and add to the well. Mix to form a dough.

Turn out the dough onto a lightly floured work surface and knead for 5-10 minutes, or until smooth and elastic. Put the dough in an oiled bowl, cover with clingfilm and leave to rise in a warm place for 1 hour, or until doubled in size.

Turn out the dough again and knead lightly for 1 minute. Slice off one-quarter of the dough, wrap in oiled clingfilm and set aside. Knead the large piece of dough lightly and shape into a ball. Transfer to the prepared mould. With a floured finger, make an indentation in the top or cut a cross with a sharp knife.

Unwrap and lightly knead the reserved dough, shape into a round, then elongate slightly to a rough pear shape. Put the pear-shaped dough on top of the larger ball of dough, narrow end downwards. Cover with lightly oiled clingfilm and leave to prove in a warm place for 1 hour. Preheat the oven to 220°C/425°F/Gas Mark 7.

Meanwhile, to make the glaze, lightly beat the egg yolk with the milk.

Brush the glaze over the top of the brioche. Bake in the preheated oven for 40-45 minutes until risen and golden brown. Transfer to a wire rack and leave to cool. Serve warm or cold.

Margarine should never be used when making brioche. Because such a large amount of butter is used, the brioche dough can be successfully frozen. If a sweeter brioche is desired increase the amount of yeast used by about 1 per cent.

PAINS AUX CHOCOLAT

Oil 2 baking sheets. Sift the flour and salt together into a warmed bowl. Stir in the yeast, sugar and milk powder. Dice 25 g/1 oz of the butter and rub into the flour mixture with your fingertips until the mixture resembles breadcrumbs. Make a well in the centre. Add the water to the well and mix to form a dough.

Turn out the dough onto a lightly floured work surface and knead for 5–10 minutes, or until smooth and elastic. Put into an oiled bowl, cover with clingfilm and leave to rise in a warm place for 1 hour, or until doubled in size. Shape the remaining butter into a rectangle 2 cm/3/4 inch thick.

Turn out the dough again and knead lightly for 1 minute. Shape into a ball and cut a cross in the centre halfway down through the dough. Roll out the edges of the dough, leaving the cross intact. Put the rectangle of butter in the centre and fold the rolled-out edges over it, pressing to seal. Roll out the dough again into a long rectangle. With the short sides facing you, fold the top one-third of the dough down to cover the middle third, then fold the bottom third up and over the top. Press down with the rolling pin to seal the edges. Wrap the dough in oiled clingfilm and chill in the refrigerator for 20 minutes. Repeat twice more, rolling from the left-hand edge each time, and finally chill for 30 minutes.

Roll out the dough into a rectangle 53 x 30 cm/21 x 12 inches. Cut lengthways into 3 strips, then widthways to make 9 equal rectangles. Put a few chocolate pieces on the short end of each rectangle. To make the glaze, beat the egg yolk with the milk. Brush some of the glaze around the edges of the rectangles. Roll up each rectangle to enclose the chocolate. Seal the edges. Transfer to the prepared baking sheets, seam-side down. Cover with oiled clingfilm and leave to prove in a warm place for 30 minutes. Preheat the oven to 200°C/400°F/Gas Mark 6.

Brush the tops of the pastries with the remaining glaze. Bake in the preheated oven for 15 minutes, or until golden. Transfer to a wire rack to cool. Serve warm.

MAKES 9

oil, for oiling

250 g/9 oz strong white bread flour, plus extra for dusting

1/2 tsp salt

1 1/2 tsp easy-blend dried yeast

1 tbsp caster sugar

2 tbsp skimmed milk powder

140 g/5 oz butter, plus extra for greasing

125 ml/4 fl oz tepid water

225 g/8 oz plain chocolate, broken into pieces

GLAZE

1 egg yolk

1 tsp milk

A butter-rich flaky exterior encases a dark chocolate centre in these classic French pastries, which are divine when freshly baked.

DOUBLE CHOCOLATE SWIRLS

These rich, chocolate buns are very quick to make for breakfast because the dough is prepared the night before.

MAKES 24

600 g/1 lb 5 oz strong white bread flour, plus extra for dusting

1/2 tsp salt

1 tsp ground cinnamon

7 g/1/6 oz easy-blend dried yeast

115 g/4 oz caster sugar

85 g/3 oz unsalted butter, melted and slightly cooled

2 large eggs, beaten, plus 1 egg, beaten, for glazing

300 ml/10 fl oz milk

oil, for oiling

6 tbsp chocolate hazelnut spread

200 g/7 oz milk chocolate, chopped

Sift the flour, salt and cinnamon together into a large warmed bowl. Stir in the yeast and sugar. Make a well in the centre. Mix the butter, the 2 eggs and milk together and add to the well. Mix to form a soft dough.

Turn out onto a lightly floured work surface and knead for 10 minutes, or until smooth and elastic. Put into a large floured bowl, cover with clingfilm and leave to rise in a warm place for 8 hours or overnight.

When you are ready to bake, preheat the oven to 220°C/425°F/Gas Mark 7. Lightly oil 2 baking sheets. Turn out the dough again and knead lightly for 1 minute. Cut the dough into 4 equal pieces. Roll out each piece into a rectangle about 2.5-cm/1-inch thick. Spread each rectangle with the chocolate hazelnut spread and scatter with the chopped chocolate. Roll up each piece like a Swiss roll, then cut into 6 pieces.

Transfer each swirl, cut-side down, to the prepared baking sheets and brush each one well with the beaten egg to glaze. Bake in the preheated oven for 20 minutes. Serve warm.

CROWN LOAF

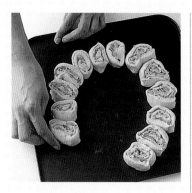

Grease a baking sheet. Sift the flour and salt together into a warmed bowl. Stir in the yeast. Rub in the butter with your fingertips until the mixture resembles breadcrumbs. Add the milk and egg and mix to form a dough.

Put the dough in a greased bowl, cover with clingfilm and leave to rise in a warm place for 40 minutes, or until doubled in size.

Turn out the dough onto a lightly floured work surface and knead lightly for 1 minute. Roll out into a rectangle 30 x 23 cm/12 x 9 inches.

To make the filling, cream the butter and brown sugar together in a bowl until light and fluffy. Stir in the nuts, ginger, mixed peel and rum.

Spread the filling over the dough, leaving a 2.5-cm/1-inch border all round. Roll up, starting from one long edge, and press down to seal. Cut into 5-cm/2-inch thick slices and arrange in a circle on the prepared baking sheet with the slices just touching. Cover and leave to prove in a warm place for 30 minutes. Preheat the oven to 190°C/375°F/Gas Mark 5.

Bake in the preheated oven for 20-30 minutes, or until golden. Meanwhile, mix the icing sugar with the lemon juice to form a thin icing.

Leave the loaf to cool slightly before drizzling with the icing. Leave the icing to set slightly before serving.

MAKES 1 LOAF

2 tbsp butter, diced, plus extra
    for greasing

225 g/8 oz strong white bread flour,
    plus extra for dusting

1/2 tsp salt

1 1/2 tsp easy-blend dried yeast

125 ml/4 fl oz tepid milk

1 egg, lightly beaten

115 g/4 oz icing sugar

2 tbsp lemon juice

FILLING

4 tbsp butter, softened

50 g/1 3/4 oz soft light brown sugar

2 tbsp chopped hazelnuts

1 tbsp chopped stem ginger

50 g/1 3/4 oz mixed peel

1 tbsp dark rum or brandy

This is a rich, sweet bread combining alcohol, nuts and fruit in a decorative wreath shape. It is ideal for serving at Christmas.

CINNAMON SWIRLS

Grease a 23-cm/9-inch square baking tin.

Sift the flour and salt together into a warmed bowl. Stir in the yeast. Rub in the butter with your fingertips until the mixture resembles breadcrumbs. Add the milk and egg and mix to form a dough.

Shape the dough into a ball, then put in a greased bowl, cover with clingfilm and leave to rise in a warm place for 40 minutes, or until doubled in size.

Turn out the dough on a lightly floured work surface and knead lightly for 1 minute. Roll out into a rectangle 30 x 23 cm/12 x 9 inches.

To make the filling, cream the butter, cinnamon and brown sugar together in a bowl until light and fluffy.

Spread the filling over the dough rectangle, leaving a 2.5-cm/1-inch border all around. Sprinkle the currants evenly over the top. Roll up, starting from one long edge, and press down to seal. Cut into 12 slices. Arrange in the prepared tin. Cover and leave to prove in a warm place for 30 minutes. Preheat the oven to 190°C/375°F/Gas Mark 5.

Bake the buns in the preheated oven for 20–30 minutes, or until well risen. Brush with the syrup and leave to cool slightly before serving.

MAKES 12

2 tbsp butter, diced, plus extra
    for greasing

225 g/8 oz strong white bread flour,
    plus extra for dusting

1/2 tsp salt

1 1/2 tsp easy-blend dried yeast

125 ml/4 fl oz tepid milk

1 egg, lightly beaten

2 tbsp maple syrup

FILLING

4 tbsp butter, softened

2 tsp ground cinnamon

50 g/1 3/4 oz soft light brown sugar

50 g/1 3/4 oz currants

These cinnamon-flavoured buns are
delicious if they are served warm
a few minutes after they come
out of the oven.

APRICOT AND WALNUT BREAD

SERVES 12

55 g/2 oz butter, diced, plus
   extra for greasing

350 g/12 oz strong white bread flour,
   plus extra for dusting

1/2 tsp salt

1 tsp golden caster sugar

2 tsp easy-blend dried yeast

115 g/4 oz ready-to-eat
   dried apricots, chopped

55 g/2 oz chopped walnuts

150 ml/5 fl oz tepid milk

75 ml/2 1/2 fl oz tepid water

1 egg, beaten

oil, for oiling

TOPPING

85 g/3 oz icing sugar

walnut halves

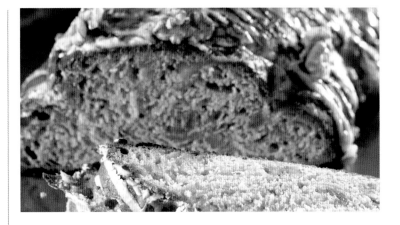

Serve this fruit bread freshly made, sliced and buttered, or leave it whole and invite guests to break off tasty morsels with their hands.

As an alternative to apricots, you can substitute glacé cherries, dried cranberries or dates.

Grease and flour a baking sheet. Sift the flour and salt together into a warmed bowl. Stir in the caster sugar and yeast. Rub in the butter with your fingertips until the mixture resembles breadcrumbs. Stir in the apricots and walnuts. Make a well in the centre. Mix the milk, water and egg together and add to the well. Mix to form a soft dough. Turn out the dough onto a lightly floured work surface and knead for 10 minutes, or until smooth and elastic. Put in an oiled bowl, cover with oiled clingfilm and leave to rise in a warm place for 2-3 hours, or until doubled in size.

Turn out the dough again and knead lightly for 1 minute. Cut into 5 equal pieces and roll each into a rope 30 cm/12 inches long. Plait 3 ropes together, pinching the ends to seal. Transfer to the prepared baking sheet. Twist the remaining 2 ropes together and put on top. Cover with oiled clingfilm and leave to prove in a warm place for 1-2 hours, or until doubled in size. Preheat the oven to 220°C/425°F/Gas Mark 7.

Bake the bread in the preheated oven for 10 minutes. Reduce the heat to 190°C/375°F/Gas Mark 5 and bake for a further 20 minutes. Transfer to a wire rack to cool. Sift the icing sugar into a bowl, stir in enough water to make a thin icing and drizzle over the loaf. Decorate with walnut halves and serve.

HOT CROSS BUNS

MAKES 12

75 g/2³/4 oz butter, melted, plus extra
    for greasing

500 g/1 lb 2 oz strong white bread
    flour, plus extra for dusting

¹/2 tsp salt

2 tsp ground mixed spice

1 tsp ground nutmeg

1 tsp ground cinnamon

1¹/2 tsp easy-blend dried yeast

50 g/1³/4 oz golden caster sugar

finely grated rind of 1 lemon

175 g/6 oz currants

75 g/2³/4 oz mixed candied peel

1 egg

225 ml/8 fl oz tepid milk

CROSSES

50 g/1³/4 oz plain flour

2 tbsp butter, diced

GLAZE

3 tbsp milk

3 tbsp golden caster sugar

Grease a baking sheet. Sift the flour, salt, mixed spice, nutmeg and cinnamon together into a large warmed bowl. Stir in the yeast, sugar, lemon rind, currants and mixed peel. Make a well in the centre. Mix the butter, egg and milk together and add to the well. Mix to form a soft dough, adding a little more milk if necessary. Turn out the dough onto a lightly floured work surface and knead for 10 minutes, or until smooth and elastic. Put the dough in a lightly greased bowl, cover with clingfilm and leave to rise in a warm place for 1¹/2-2 hours, or until doubled in size.

Turn out the dough again and knead lightly for 1 minute. Cut the dough into 12 equal pieces and shape each piece into a ball. Transfer to the prepared baking sheet and flatten slightly. Cover loosely with greased clingfilm and leave to prove in a warm place for 45 minutes, or until doubled in size. Preheat the oven to 220°C/425°F/Gas Mark 7.

To make the crosses, sift the flour into a bowl. Rub in the butter with your fingertips until the mixture resembles breadcrumbs. Stir in a little cold water, about 1 tablespoon, and mix to form a dough. Cut the dough into 24 equal pieces and form into strips about 18 cm/7 inches long.

To make the glaze, gently heat the milk and sugar in a small saucepan until the sugar has dissolved. Brush a little glaze over the buns, then form crosses with the pastry strips. Bake in the preheated oven for 15-20 minutes until golden. Brush with the remaining glaze and bake for a further 1 minute. Transfer to a wire rack to cool.

There is nothing more tempting than the aroma of spicy hot cross buns straight from the oven.

CHELSEA BUNS

Grease an 18-cm/7-inch square cake tin. Sift the flour and salt together into a warmed bowl, then stir in the yeast and caster sugar. Rub in the butter with your fingertips until the mixture resembles breadcrumbs. Make a well in the centre. Mix the milk and egg together and add to the well. Mix to form a soft dough. Turn out the dough on a lightly floured work surface and knead for 5–10 minutes, or until smooth and elastic. Put in an oiled bowl, cover with clingfilm and leave to rise in a warm place for 1 hour, or until doubled in size.

Turn out the dough again and knead lightly for 1 minute. Roll out into a rectangle 30 x 23 cm/12 x 9 inches.

To make the filling, mix the muscovado sugar, dried fruit and mixed spice together in a bowl. Spread the dough with the butter and sprinkle the fruit mixture on top. Roll up, starting from one long edge. Cut into 9 slices and arrange, cut-side up, in the prepared tin. Cover with oiled clingfilm and leave to prove in a warm place for 45 minutes. Preheat the oven to 190°C/375°F/Gas Mark 5.

Bake the buns in the preheated oven for 30 minutes, or until golden. Leave to cool in the tin for 10 minutes, then transfer, in one piece, to a wire rack and leave to cool completely. Sift the icing sugar into a bowl and stir in enough water to make a thin glaze. Brush over the buns and leave to set. Pull the buns apart to serve.

MAKES 9

2 tbsp butter, diced, plus extra
   for greasing
225 g/8 oz strong white bread flour,
   plus extra for dusting
1/2 tsp salt
1 1/2 tsp easy-blend dried yeast
1 tsp golden caster sugar
125 ml/4 fl oz tepid milk
1 egg, beaten
oil, for oiling
85 g/3 oz icing sugar

FILLING

55 g/2 oz light muscovado sugar
115 g/4 oz luxury mixed dried fruit
1 tsp ground mixed spice
4 tbsp butter, softened

These sweet and sticky buns, with a hint of spice, are irresistible. A perfect treat to serve at any time of day!

DOUGHNUTS IN HONEY SYRUP

SERVES 6

300 g/10^1/$_2$ oz strong white
  bread flour
1 tsp salt
finely grated rind of 1 orange
1^1/$_2$ tsp easy-blend dried yeast
300 ml/10 fl oz tepid water, plus
  1 tbsp
125 ml/4 fl oz Greek honey
1 tsp lemon juice
sunflower oil, for deep-frying
ground cinnamon, for sprinkling

These little fritters are delicious served as a dessert or as an afternoon snack - especially for children. They are sold in every café throughout Greece.

Put the flour, salt and orange rind in the bowl of an electric mixer fitted with a dough hook and sprinkle in the yeast. Gradually add the 300 ml/ 10 fl oz water and whisk for 10 minutes to form a thick batter. Alternatively, make the batter in a large bowl using a hand-held electric whisk or balloon whisk. Cover the bowl with a clean tea towel and leave in a warm place for 2 hours, or until risen with lots of bubbles.

Meanwhile, to make the honey syrup, put the honey, lemon juice and 1 tablespoon water in a saucepan and simmer until combined. Set aside.

When the batter has risen, heat the oil in a deep-fat fryer or deep saucepan to 180-190°C/350-375°F, or until a cube of bread browns in 30 seconds. Using 2 teaspoons (one to scoop and one to push), dip the spoons in cold water to prevent the batter from sticking and drop small amounts of the batter into the hot oil. Cook about 5 at a time for 2-3 minutes, turning with a slotted spoon, until puffed up and golden brown. Remove with the slotted spoon and drain on kitchen paper.

Serve about 5 hot doughnuts per person, spoon over the warm honey syrup and sprinkle with cinnamon.

CHURROS

Heat the water, butter, brown sugar, orange rind, if using, and salt in a heavy-based saucepan over a medium heat until the butter has melted.

Add the flour, all at once, the cinnamon and vanilla extract, then remove from the heat and beat rapidly until the mixture pulls away from the side of the saucepan.

Leave to cool slightly, then beat in the eggs, one at a time, beating well after each addition, until the mixture is thick and smooth. Spoon into a piping bag fitted with a wide star nozzle.

Heat the oil for deep-frying in a deep-fat fryer or deep saucepan to 180–190°C/350–375°F, or until a cube of bread browns in 30 seconds. Pipe 13-cm/5-inch lengths about 7.5 cm/3 inches apart into the oil. Cook for 4 minutes, or until golden brown. Remove with a slotted spoon and drain on kitchen paper.

Dust the churros with caster sugar and cinnamon and serve either hot from the pan or cooled to room temperature.

SERVES 4

225 ml/8 fl oz water

100 g/3½ oz butter or lard, diced

2 tbsp soft light brown sugar

finely grated rind of 1 small orange
   (optional)

pinch of salt

175 g/6 oz plain flour, sifted

1 tsp ground cinnamon, plus extra
   for dusting

1 tsp vanilla extract

2 eggs

vegetable oil, for deep-frying

caster sugar, for dusting

This Mexican-style doughnut looks rather more appealing than its traditional relative, since the dough is piped into lengths, which twist into a variety of interesting shapes when deep-fried. Churros go equally well with a cup of hot chocolate or a coffee.

STOLLEN

Oil a baking sheet.

Put the currants, raisins, mixed peel and cherries in a bowl. Stir in the rum and set aside. Put the butter, milk and caster sugar in a saucepan and heat gently until the sugar has dissolved and the butter has just melted. Leave to cool until hand-hot. Sift the flour, salt, nutmeg and cinnamon together into a bowl. Crush the cardamom seeds with a pestle in a mortar and add to the flour mixture. Stir in the yeast. Make a well in the centre and add the milk mixture, lemon rind and egg. Beat to form a soft dough.

Turn out the dough onto a lightly floured work surface. With floured hands, knead the dough for 5-10 minutes – it will be quite sticky, so add more flour if necessary. Knead the soaked fruit and almonds into the dough until just combined. Return the dough to the clean, lightly oiled bowl. Cover with clingfilm and leave to rise in a warm place for up to 3 hours, or until doubled in size. Turn out the dough again and knead lightly for 1-2 minutes. Roll out into a 25-cm/10-inch square.

Roll the marzipan into a sausage shape slightly shorter than the length of the dough and position down the centre. Fold one side over to cover the marzipan. Repeat with the other side, overlapping in the centre. Seal the ends. Transfer the roll, seam-side down, to the prepared baking sheet. Cover with oiled clingfilm and leave to prove in a warm place until doubled in size. Preheat the oven to 190°C/375°F/Gas Mark 5.

Bake the stollen in the preheated oven for 40 minutes, or until golden and it sounds hollow when tapped on the base. Brush the hot stollen generously with melted butter and dredge heavily with icing sugar. Transfer to a wire rack and leave to cool completely.

Stollen is a spiced German fruit bread with a marzipan filling, which is traditionally served at Christmas.

SERVES 10

oil, for oiling

85 g/3 oz currants

55 g/2 oz raisins

35 g/1^{1}/4 oz mixed peel

55 g/2 oz glacé cherries, rinsed, dried and quartered

2 tbsp dark rum

4 tbsp butter, plus extra, melted, for brushing

175 ml/6 fl oz milk

3 tbsp golden caster sugar

375 g/13 oz strong white bread flour, plus extra for dusting

^{1}/2 tsp salt

^{1}/2 tsp ground nutmeg

^{1}/2 tsp ground cinnamon

seeds from 3 green cardamom pods

2 tsp easy-blend dried yeast

finely grated rind of 1 lemon

1 egg, beaten

40 g/1^{1}/2 oz flaked almonds

175 g/6 oz ready-made marzipan

sifted icing sugar, for dusting

BARM BRACKE

SERVES 15

650 g/1 lb 7 oz strong white bread flour, plus extra for dusting

1 tsp ground mixed spice

1 tsp salt

2 tsp easy-blend dried yeast

55 g/2 oz golden caster sugar

300 ml/10 fl oz tepid milk, plus extra for glazing

150 ml/5 fl oz tepid water

vegetable oil, for brushing

55 g/2 oz butter, softened, plus extra for greasing

325 g/11^1/2 oz mixed dried fruit

Sift the flour, mixed spice and salt into a warmed bowl, then stir in the yeast and 1 tablespoon of the caster sugar. Make a well in the centre and pour in the milk and water. Mix well, gradually incorporating the dry ingredients to make a sticky dough. Place on a lightly floured work surface and knead the dough until no longer sticky. Brush a clean, warmed bowl with oil, place the dough in the bowl, cover with clingfilm and leave in a warm place for 1 hour, or until doubled in size.

Turn the dough out on to a floured work surface and knead lightly for 1 minute. Add the butter and mixed fruit to the dough and work them in well. Return the dough to the bowl, replace the clingfilm and leave to rise for 30 minutes. Grease a 23-cm/9-inch round cake tin. Shape the dough into a neat round and fit in the tin. Cover and leave in a warm place until it has risen to the top of the tin. Preheat the oven to 200°C/400°F/Gas Mark 6.

Brush the top of the loaf lightly with milk and bake in the preheated oven for 15 minutes. Cover the loaf with foil, reduce the oven temperature to 180°C/350°F/Gas Mark 4 and bake for 45 minutes, or until the bread is golden and sounds hollow when tapped on the bottom. Transfer to a wire rack to cool.

This Irish spiced bread was traditionally baked with a wedding ring thrown into the mixture in the belief that whoever found the ring would be married within the year.

TROPICAL FRUIT BREAD

Grease a baking sheet.

Sift the flour, salt and ginger together into a large warmed bowl. Stir in the bran, yeast and sugar. Rub in the butter with your fingertips until the mixture resembles breadcrumbs. Add the water and mix to form a dough.

Turn out the dough on a lightly floured work surface and knead for 5-10 minutes, or until smooth and elastic. Put the dough in a greased bowl, cover with clingfilm and leave to rise in a warm place for 30 minutes, or until doubled in size.

Turn out the dough again and knead in the pineapple, mango and coconut. Shape into a round and transfer to the prepared baking sheet. Score the top with the back of a knife. Cover with clingfilm and leave to prove in a warm place for 30 minutes. Preheat the oven to 220ºC/425ºF/Gas Mark 7.

Brush the loaf with the beaten egg and sprinkle with coconut. Bake in the preheated oven for 30 minutes, or until golden brown.

Transfer the bread to a wire rack and leave to cool before serving.

MAKES 1 LOAF

2 tbsp butter, diced, plus extra
for greasing
375 g/13 oz strong white bread flour,
plus extra for dusting
1/2 tsp salt
1/2 tsp ground ginger
25 g/1 oz bran
1 1/2 tsp easy-blend dried yeast
2 tbsp soft light brown sugar
250 ml/9 fl oz tepid water
55 g/2 oz glacé pineapple, chopped
finely
2 tbsp finely chopped dried mango
70 g/2 1/2 oz grated coconut, toasted,
plus extra for sprinkling
1 egg, lightly beaten

The flavours in this fruit bread will bring a touch of sunshine to your table, whatever the time of year. To test the bread after the second proving, gently prod the dough with your finger – it should spring back if it has proved enough.

MANGO TWIST BREAD

This is a sweet bread that has puréed mango mixed into the dough, resulting in a moist loaf with an exotic flavour.

MAKES 1 LOAF

40 g/1¹/₂ oz butter, diced, plus extra
    for greasing

450 g/1 lb strong white bread flour,
    plus extra for dusting

1 tsp salt

1 tsp ground ginger

1 ¹/₂ tsp easy-blend dried yeast

50 g/1³/₄ oz soft light brown sugar

1 small mango, peeled, stoned and
    blended to a purée

225 ml/8 fl oz tepid water

2 tbsp honey

115 g/4 oz sultanas

1 egg, lightly beaten

icing sugar, for dusting

Grease a baking sheet. Sift the flour, salt and ginger together into a large warmed bowl. Stir in the yeast and brown sugar. Rub in the butter with your fingertips until the mixture resembles breadcrumbs. Stir in the mango purée, water and honey and mix to form a dough.

Turn out the dough onto a lightly floured work surface and knead for 5-10 minutes, or until smooth and elastic. Put the dough in a greased bowl, cover with clingfilm and leave to rise in a warm place for 1 hour, or until doubled in size.

Turn out the dough again and knead in the sultanas. Shape the dough into 2 sausage shapes, each 25 cm/10 inches long. Carefully twist the 2 pieces together and pinch the ends to seal. Transfer to the prepared baking sheet, cover and leave to prove in a warm place for 40 minutes. Preheat the oven to 220°C/425°F/Gas Mark 7.

Brush the loaf with the beaten egg. Bake in the preheated oven for 30 minutes, or until golden brown. Transfer to a wire rack and leave to cool. Dust with icing sugar before serving.

FRUIT AND NUT LOAF

Lightly grease a baking sheet. Sift the flour and salt together into a warmed bowl. Rub in the margarine with your fingertips until the mixture resembles breadcrumbs. Stir in the sugar, dried fruit, nuts and yeast.

Warm the orange juice in a saucepan over a low heat, but do not let it boil. Stir into the flour mixture with the yogurt. Mix to form a dough.

Turn out the dough on a lightly floured work surface and knead for 5-10 minutes, or until smooth and elastic. Shape into a round and transfer to the prepared baking sheet. Cover with a clean tea towel and leave to rise in a warm place for 1 hour, or until doubled in size. Preheat the oven to 220°C/425°F/Gas Mark 7.

Bake the loaf in the preheated oven for 35-40 minutes until it sounds hollow when tapped on the base. Transfer to a wire rack and brush the top of the warm loaf with the apricot jam. Leave to cool before serving.

MAKES 1 LOAF

1 tbsp margarine, plus extra
  for greasing

280 g/10 oz strong white bread flour,
  plus extra for dusting

1/2 tsp salt

2 tbsp soft light brown sugar

115 g/4 oz sultanas

55 g/2 oz ready-to-eat dried
  apricots, chopped

75 g/2 3/4 oz chopped hazelnuts

2 tsp easy-blend dried yeast

6 tbsp orange juice

6 tbsp natural yogurt

2 tbsp sieved apricot jam

This fruit bread may be served warm or cold, perhaps spread with a little butter, or topped with apricot jam.

CHOCOLATE BREAD

Lightly grease a 900-g/2-lb loaf tin.

Sift the flour, salt and cocoa powder together into a large bowl. Stir in the yeast and sugar. Make a well in the centre. Add the oil and water to the well and mix to form a dough.

Turn out the dough on a lightly floured work surface and knead for 5-10 minutes, or until smooth and elastic. Put the dough in an oiled bowl, cover with clingfilm and leave to rise in a warm place for 1 hour, or until doubled in size.

Turn out the dough again and knead lightly for 1 minute. Shape into a loaf. Transfer the dough to the prepared tin, cover and leave to prove in a warm place for 30 minutes. Preheat the oven to 200°C/400°F/ Gas Mark 6.

MAKES 1 LOAF

butter, for greasing and to serve

450 g/1 lb strong white bread flour,
   plus extra for dusting

1 tsp salt

25 g/1 oz cocoa powder

1¹/₂ tsp easy-blend dried yeast

2 tbsp soft light brown sugar

1 tbsp oil, plus extra for oiling

300 ml/10 fl oz tepid water

Bake the loaf in the preheated oven for 25-30 minutes, or until it sounds hollow when tapped on the base. Transfer the loaf to a wire rack and leave to cool completely. Cut into thick slices and serve with butter.

For the chocoholics among us, this bread is not only great fun to make, it also has a fantastic chocolate flavour. This bread can be sliced and spread with butter, or it can be lightly toasted.

breads

One of the most therapeutic of all baking methods must surely be the kneading of bread dough. The following pages give a flavour of the many types and shapes of bread enjoyed around the world. The recipes include Italian and Indian breads and breads with extra ingredients such as yogurt or potato. So whether it is rolls, sticks, loaves or flatbreads that take your fancy, rise to the occasion and enjoy the mesmerizing smell of freshly cooked bread.

WHITE BREAD

Grease a 900-g/2-lb loaf tin or 2 baking sheets.

Sift the flour and salt together into a large warmed bowl. Stir in the yeast. Make a well in the centre. Add the oil and water to the well and mix to form a soft dough.

Turn out the dough onto a lightly floured work surface and knead for 5-10 minutes, or until smooth and elastic. Put the dough in an oiled bowl, cover with clingfilm and leave to rise in a warm place for 1 hour, or until doubled in size.

Turn out the dough again and knead lightly. For a loaf, shape into a rectangle the length of the tin and 3 times the width. With the long sides facing you, fold the top one-third down to cover the middle third, then fold the bottom one-third up and over the top and press together. Transfer to the prepared tin, join-side down. Alternatively, to make rolls, cut the dough into 8 equal pieces, shape each piece into a round and space well apart on the prepared baking sheets. Dust with a little extra flour for a softer crust. Cover and leave to prove in a warm place for 30 minutes, or until the loaf is well risen above the tin or the rolls have doubled in size. Preheat the oven to 230ºC/450ºF/Gas Mark 8.

If baking a loaf, bake in the centre of the preheated oven for 25-30 minutes, or until it sounds hollow when tapped on the base. If the top is browning too much, reduce the temperature a little. For the rolls, bake for 15-20 minutes, swapping the baking sheets around halfway through the baking time.

Transfer to a wire rack and leave to cool. Eat as fresh as possible.

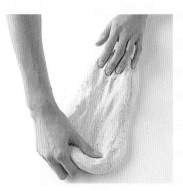

MAKES 1 LARGE LOAF OR 8 ROLLS

butter, for greasing

450 g/1 lb strong white bread flour, plus extra for dusting

1 tsp salt

1¹/₂ tsp easy-blend dried yeast

1 tbsp vegetable oil, plus extra for oiling

350 ml/12 fl oz tepid water

Bread is the staple food of many countries. In addition to the wide popularity of white bread, a variety of flours is used for making good-quality alternative breads, including organic, Granary and wholemeal flours.

PLAITED POPPY SEED BREAD

MAKES 1 LOAF

2 tbsp sunflower oil, plus extra
   for oiling

225 g/8 oz strong white bread flour,
   plus extra for dusting

2 tbsp skimmed milk powder

1 tsp salt

1¼ tbsp sugar

175 ml/6 fl oz hand-hot water

1 tsp easy-blend dried yeast

5 tbsp poppy seeds

TOPPING

1 egg yolk

1 tbsp milk

1 tbsp caster sugar

2 tbsp poppy seeds

Oil a baking sheet. Sift the flour into a large bowl, and add the milk powder, salt and sugar. Pour in the water and oil. Make an indentation in the flour with your finger and add the yeast to it.

Lightly flour a work surface. Knock the dough back gently and knead lightly for 1-2 minutes. Add the poppy seeds.

Divide the dough into 3 equal pieces and shape each piece into a rope about 25-30 cm/10-12 inches long. Place the ropes side by side and pinch them together at one end. Plait the dough, and pinch the other end together, tucking it underneath. Place the plait on the baking sheet, cover with lightly oiled clingfilm and set aside in a warm place for about 30 minutes to rise. Preheat the oven to 200°C/400°F/Gas Mark 6.

To make the topping, lightly beat the egg yolk with the milk and caster sugar to combine. Remove the clingfilm from the plait, brush the top with the egg glaze and sprinkle over poppy seeds. Bake in the preheated oven for 30-35 minutes, until the loaf is golden on the top and sounds hollow when tapped on the base. Transfer to a wire rack and leave to cool.

If you are not used to plaiting, try practising on the kitchen table with three tightly rolled-up tea towels.

MIXED SEED BREAD

Grease a 900-g/2-lb loaf tin. Sift the flours and salt together into a large warmed bowl. Stir in the yeast, sugar, milk powder and seeds. Make a well in the centre. Mix the water, oil and lemon juice together and add to the well. Mix to form a dough.

Turn out the dough onto a lightly floured work surface and knead for 5–10 minutes, or until smooth and elastic. Put the dough into an oiled bowl, cover with clingfilm and leave to rise in a warm place for 1 hour, or until doubled in size.

Turn out the dough again and knead lightly. Shape into a loaf and transfer to the prepared tin. Cover and leave to prove in a warm place for 30 minutes. Preheat the oven to 220°C/425°F/Gas Mark 7.

To make the topping, lightly beat the egg white with the water. Brush over the top of the loaf, then gently press the seeds all over the top. Bake in the preheated oven for 25–30 minutes, or until it sounds hollow when tapped on the base. Transfer to a wire rack and leave to cool.

MAKES 1 LOAF

butter, for greasing

375 g/13 oz strong white bread flour,
   plus extra for dusting

125 g/4^{1}/2 oz rye flour

1^{1}/2 tsp salt

1 tsp easy-blend dried yeast

1 tbsp light brown sugar

1^{1}/2 tbsp skimmed milk powder

1 tsp caraway seeds

^{1}/2 tsp poppy seeds

^{1}/2 tsp sesame seeds

300 ml/10 fl oz tepid water

1^{1}/2 tbsp sunflower oil, plus extra
   for oiling

2 tsp lemon juice

TOPPING

1 egg white

1 tbsp water

1 tbsp sunflower or
   pumpkin seeds

FRENCH STICK

Lightly oil a baking sheet.

Sift the flour and salt together into a large warmed bowl. Stir in the yeast. Make a well in the centre. Add the water to the well and mix to form a soft dough.

Turn out the dough onto a lightly floured work surface and knead for 5-10 minutes, or until smooth and elastic. Put the dough in an oiled bowl, cover with clingfilm and leave to rise in a warm place for 1 hour, or until doubled in size.

Turn out the dough again and knead lightly. Cut the dough in half. Shape each half into a ball. Roll out each ball into a rectangle 7.5 x 20 cm/3 x 8 inches. With the long sides of one rectangle facing you, fold one-third down to cover the middle third, then fold the bottom third up and over the top and press together. Set aside to rest while you repeat with the second rectangle. Repeat twice more with each rectangle, leaving to rest between each folding.

Lightly flour and pleat 2 clean tea towels. Gently roll and stretch each piece of dough, in turn, into a stick about 30 cm/12 inches long. Put each baguette between the pleats of a tea towel to support it and cover with lightly oiled clingfilm. Leave to prove in a warm place for 30-40 minutes. Preheat the oven to 230°C/450°F/Gas Mark 8.

Gently roll the loaves from the tea towels onto the prepared baking sheet, spaced well apart. Make several diagonal slashes on the tops with a sharp knife. Spray the preheated oven with water and bake the loaves for 15-20 minutes until crusty and golden. Transfer to a wire rack and leave to cool. Eat as fresh as possible.

MAKES 2

oil, for oiling

450 g/1 lb strong white bread flour, plus extra for dusting

1¹/₂ tsp salt

1¹/₂ tsp easy-blend dried yeast

325 ml/11 fl oz tepid water

The first sign of quality in a baguette is a hard crust of a rich, dark caramel colour. The texture of a good baguette should be moist and slightly chewy.

WHITE BAPS

MAKES 10

oil, for oiling

450 g/1 lb strong white bread flour,
  plus extra for dusting

1¹/₂ tsp salt

1 tsp easy-blend dried yeast

2 tsp caster sugar

140 ml/4¹/₂ fl oz tepid water

140 ml/4¹/₂ fl oz tepid milk

milk, for glazing

Lightly oil 2 baking sheets.

Sift the flour and salt together into a large warmed bowl. Stir in the yeast and sugar. Make a well in the centre. Add the water and milk to the well and mix to form a soft dough.

Turn out the dough onto a lightly floured work surface and knead for 5-10 minutes, or until smooth and elastic. Put the dough in an oiled bowl, cover with clingfilm and leave to rise in a warm place for 1 hour, or until doubled in size.

Turn out the dough again and knead lightly.

Cut the dough into 10 equal pieces, shape each piece into a ball, then roll out into a 10-cm/4-inch long oval. Space the ovals well apart on the prepared baking sheets and cover with lightly oiled clingfilm. Leave to prove in a warm place for 30 minutes. Preheat the oven to 200°C/400°F/Gas Mark 6.

Gently press the centre of each bap with 2 fingers to release any large air bubbles, then brush the tops with milk and dust with a little extra flour for a softer crust.

Bake in the preheated oven for 15-20 minutes, or until lightly browned. Transfer the baps to wire racks and leave to cool slightly. Serve warm.

You could shape your dough into a log and use a stiff spatula to divide it into equal portions. To be exact, weigh each piece of dough so the baps are the same size.

ENGLISH MUFFINS

MAKES 10-12

450 g/1 lb strong white bread flour,
   plus extra for dusting

2 x 7 g/^{1}/$_6$ oz easy-blend dried yeast

250 ml/9 fl oz tepid water

125 ml/4 fl oz natural yogurt

^{1}/$_2$ tsp salt

50 g/1^3/$_4$ oz fine semolina

vegetable oil, for brushing

TO SERVE

butter

jam (optional)

Lightly flour a baking sheet. Mix the yeast with half the water in a bowl until it has dissolved. Add the remaining water and the yogurt and mix well. Sift the flour and salt together into a large warmed bowl. Make a well in the centre. Add the yeast mixture to the well and mix to form a soft dough.

Turn out the dough onto a lightly floured work surface and knead for 5-10 minutes until smooth and elastic. Return to the bowl, cover with clingfilm and leave to rise in a warm place for 30-40 minutes, or until doubled in size.

Turn out the dough again and knead lightly. Roll out to a thickness of 2 cm/3/4 inch. Using a 7.5-cm/3-inch cutter, cut into 10-12 rounds and scatter the semolina over each muffin. Transfer to the prepared baking sheet, cover and leave to prove in a warm place for 30-40 minutes.

Heat a griddle or a large frying pan over a medium-high heat. Lightly brush with oil. Add half the muffins and cook for 7-8 minutes on each side, taking care not to burn them. Repeat with the remaining muffins.

Serve freshly cooked with lots of butter. Muffins can be kept for up to 2 days in an airtight container. To reheat, split them across the centre and quickly toast before serving with butter, and jam, if you like.

If you do not have a round cutter, use a large mug to cut the muffins out of the dough.

HARVEST LOAF

Oil a 900-g/2-lb loaf tin. Sift the flour and salt together into a warmed bowl. Stir in the yeast, sugar and milk powder. Make a well in the centre. Add the oil and water to the well and mix to form a soft dough.

Turn out the dough onto a lightly floured work surface and knead for 5-10 minutes, or until smooth and elastic. Put in an oiled bowl, cover with clingfilm and leave to rise in a warm place for 1 hour, or until doubled in size.

Turn out the dough again and knead lightly. Shape into a loaf and transfer to the prepared tin. Cover and leave to prove in a warm place for 30 minutes. Preheat the oven to 220°C/425°F/Gas Mark 7.

Bake in the preheated oven for 25-30 minutes, or until it sounds hollow when tapped on the base. Transfer to a wire rack and leave to cool.

MAKES 1 LOAF

1¹/₂ tbsp sunflower oil, plus extra
   for oiling

225 g/8 oz strong wholemeal bread
   flour, plus extra for dusting

1 tsp salt

1 tsp easy-blend dried yeast

2 tbsp soft light brown sugar

1 tbsp skimmed milk powder

175 ml/6 fl oz tepid water

You can tell if the loaf is ready, because it should sound hollow when you tap it with your knuckles.

WHOLEMEAL YOGURT BREAD

MAKES 1 LOAF

1 tbsp sunflower oil, plus extra
    for oiling

200 g/7 oz strong white bread flour,
    plus extra for dusting

150 g/5$^{1}/_{2}$ oz strong wholemeal
    bread flour

1 tsp salt

25 g/1 oz wheat bran

$^{3}/_{4}$ tsp easy-blend dried yeast

150 ml/5 fl oz tepid water

125 ml/4 fl oz natural yogurt, at
    room temperature

1 tbsp black treacle or golden syrup

The flour used should be at room temperature. If your flour feels cold, try warming it up in a low oven for a few minutes.

Oil a baking sheet. Sift the flours and salt together into a warmed bowl. Stir in the bran and yeast. Make a well in the centre. Mix the water, yogurt, oil and treacle together and add to the well. Mix to form a soft dough.

Turn out the dough onto a lightly floured work surface and knead for 5-10 minutes, or until smooth and elastic. Put in an oiled bowl, cover with clingfilm and leave to rise in a warm place for 1 hour, or until doubled in size.

Turn out the dough again and knead lightly. Shape into a round and transfer to the prepared baking sheet. Cover and leave to prove in a warm place for 30 minutes. Preheat the oven to 220°C/425°F/Gas Mark 7.

Bake in the preheated oven for 25-30 minutes, or until it sounds hollow when tapped on the base. Transfer to a wire rack and leave to cool.

OATMEAL AND POTATO BREAD

Floury potatoes have a soft, dry texture once cooked. Popular varieties include King Edward and Maris Piper.

MAKES 1 LOAF

oil, for oiling

225 g/8 oz floury potatoes
   (peeled weight)

500 g/1 lb 2 oz strong white bread
   flour, plus extra for dusting

1¹/₂ tsp salt

40 g/1¹/₂ oz butter, diced

1¹/₂ tsp easy-blend dried yeast

1¹/₂ tbsp soft dark brown sugar

3 tbsp rolled oats

2 tbsp skimmed milk powder

210 ml/7¹/₂ fl oz tepid water

TOPPING

1 tbsp water

1 tbsp rolled oats

Oil a 900-g/2-lb loaf tin. Put the potatoes in a large saucepan, add water to cover and bring to the boil. Cook for 20-25 minutes until tender. Drain, then mash until smooth. Leave to cool.

Sift the flour and salt into a warmed bowl. Rub in the butter with your fingertips. Stir in the yeast, sugar, oats and milk powder. Mix in the mashed potato, then add the water and mix to a soft dough.

Turn out the dough onto a lightly floured work surface and knead for 5-10 minutes, or until smooth and elastic. Put the dough in an oiled bowl, cover with clingfilm and leave to rise in a warm place for 1 hour, or until doubled in size.

Turn out the dough again and knead lightly. Shape into a loaf and transfer to the prepared tin. Cover and leave to prove in a warm place for 30 minutes. Preheat the oven to 220°C/425°F/Gas Mark 7.

Brush the surface of the loaf with the water and carefully sprinkle over the oats. Bake in the preheated oven for 25-30 minutes, or until it sounds hollow when tapped on the base. Transfer to a wire rack and leave to cool slightly. Serve warm.

IRISH SODA BREAD

Preheat the oven to 220ºC/425ºF/Gas Mark 7. Oil a baking sheet.

Sift the flour, salt and bicarbonate of soda together into a large bowl. Make a well in the centre. Add most of the buttermilk to the well and, using your hands, mix to form a dough. The dough should be very soft but not too wet. Add the remaining buttermilk if necessary.

Turn out the dough onto a lightly floured work surface and knead lightly. Shape into a 20-cm/8-inch round.

Transfer the loaf to the prepared baking sheet, cut a cross in the top and bake in the preheated oven for 25–30 minutes, or until it sounds hollow when tapped on the base. Transfer to a wire rack and leave to cool slightly. Eat while still warm. Soda bread is always best eaten the same day as it is baked.

MAKES 1 LOAF

oil, for oiling

450 g/1 lb plain flour, plus extra
   for dusting

1 tsp salt

1 tsp bicarbonate of soda

400 ml/14 fl oz buttermilk

Soda bread has been a staple in Ireland for many centuries. It is a bread made without yeast, the raising agent being bicarbonate of soda mixed with buttermilk. It is simple to make, needs very little kneading and no time at all for rising. The loaves are cut on the top into a cross shape to help the bread rise and, according to Irish folklore, to let the devils (or the fairies) out. Soda bread can be made with brown or white flour or a mixture of the two and is a wonderful partner for cheese and an ideal accompaniment to soup.

RYE AND SEED BREAD

Oil a 900-g/2-lb loaf tin. Sift all the flours and salt together into a large warmed bowl. Stir in the yeast, breadcrumbs, bran, cocoa powder and caraway seeds. Make a well in the centre. Mix the water, oil and treacle together, add to the well and mix to form a soft dough.

Turn out the dough onto a lightly floured work surface and knead for 5–10 minutes, or until smooth and elastic. Put the dough in an oiled bowl, cover with clingfilm and leave to rise in a warm place for 1 hour, or until doubled in size.

Turn out the dough again and knead lightly. Shape into a loaf and transfer to the prepared tin. Cover and leave to prove in a warm place for 30 minutes. Preheat the oven to 220°C/425°F/Gas Mark 7.

Bake the loaf in the preheated oven for 25–30 minutes, or until it sounds hollow when tapped on the base. Transfer to a wire rack and leave to cool.

MAKES 1 LOAF

2 tbsp sunflower oil, plus extra
   for oiling
250 g/9 oz strong white bread flour,
   plus extra for dusting
140 g/5 oz rye flour
85 g/3 oz plain wholemeal flour
$1^1/_2$ tsp salt
$^1/_2$ tsp easy-blend dried yeast
75 g/$2^3/_4$ oz dried breadcrumbs
3 tbsp oat bran
$1^1/_2$ tbsp cocoa powder
2 tsp caraway seeds
360 ml/$12^1/_2$ fl oz tepid water
$2^1/_2$ tbsp black treacle

Made from a cereal grass, rye flour has less gluten than all-purpose or wholemeal flour. It is heavier and darker in colour than most flours and produces dense bread. The most common form is medium rye flour, available in supermarkets.

BREADSTICKS

Lightly oil 2 baking sheets.

Sift the flour and salt together into a warmed bowl. Stir in the yeast. Make a well in the centre. Add the water and oil to the well and mix to form a soft dough.

Turn out the dough onto a lightly floured work surface and knead for 5-10 minutes, or until smooth and elastic. Put the dough in an oiled bowl, cover with clingfilm and leave to rise in a warm place for 1 hour, or until doubled in size.

Turn out the dough again and knead lightly. Roll out into a rectangle 23 x 20 cm/9 x 8 inches. Cut the dough into 3 strips, each 20 cm/ 8 inches long, then cut each strip across into 10 equal pieces.

Gently roll and stretch each piece of dough into a stick about 30 cm/ 12 inches long. Spread the sesame seeds out on a large, shallow plate or tray. Roll each breadstick in the sesame seeds to coat, then space well apart on the prepared baking sheets. Brush with oil, cover with clingfilm and leave to prove in a warm place for 15 minutes. Preheat the oven to 200°C/400°F/Gas Mark 6.

Bake the breadsticks in the preheated oven for 10 minutes. Turn over and bake for a further 5-10 minutes until golden. Transfer to a wire rack and leave to cool.

MAKES 30

3 tbsp olive oil, plus extra for oiling and brushing

350 g/12 oz strong white bread flour, plus extra for dusting

$1^{1}/2$ tsp salt

$1^{1}/2$ tsp easy-blend dried yeast

200 ml/7 fl oz tepid water

sesame seeds, for coating

Breadsticks are the ideal accompaniment to soup or salad. For added flavour, try adding some Parmesan cheese and fresh or dried Rosemary to your breadstick mix before making the dough.

FOCACCIA WITH MOZZARELLA AND ROSEMARY

This Italian flatbread is extremely versatile. As well as baking it plain, you could bake it with toppings such as cheese, onion, roasted peppers and sundried tomatoes.

MAKES 1 LOAF

1 tbsp olive oil, plus extra for oiling

350 g/12 oz strong white bread flour,
    plus extra for dusting

$1/2$ tsp salt

1 tsp easy-blend dried yeast

1 tsp sugar

210 ml/$7^1/2$ fl oz tepid water

140 g/5 oz mozzarella cheese, grated

TOPPING

2 tbsp olive oil

fresh rosemary sprigs

coarse sea salt

Lightly oil a 25-cm/10-inch round shallow cake tin.

Sift the flour and salt together into a warmed bowl. Stir in the yeast and sugar. Make a well in the centre. Add the water and oil to the well and mix to form a soft dough.

Turn out the dough onto a lightly floured work surface and knead for 5-10 minutes, or until smooth and elastic. Put the dough in an oiled bowl, cover with clingfilm and leave to rise in a warm place for 1 hour, or until doubled in size.

Turn out the dough again and knead lightly. Flatten the dough, then sprinkle over the mozzarella cheese and gently knead in. Shape into a ball, flatten slightly, then roll out into a 25-cm/10-inch round. Transfer to the prepared tin, cover with lightly oiled clingfilm and leave to prove in a warm place for 20 minutes.

Make deep indentations all over the surface of the dough with your fingers. Cover with lightly oiled clingfilm and leave to prove in a warm place for a further 15 minutes. Preheat the oven to 200°C/400°F/Gas Mark 6.

To make the topping, drizzle the oil all over the surface of the dough, then sprinkle with rosemary sprigs and sea salt. Bake in the preheated oven for 20-25 minutes until golden. Transfer to a wire rack and leave to cool slightly. Serve warm.

CIABATTA WITH TOMATO AND BASIL

MAKES 2 LOAVES

ITALIAN SPONGE

175 g/6 oz strong white bread flour

1/2 tsp easy-blend dried yeast

200 ml/7 fl oz tepid water

DOUGH

325 g/11 1/2 oz strong white bread
   flour, plus extra for dusting

1 1/2 tsp salt

1/4 tsp easy-blend dried yeast

1/2 tsp sugar

200 ml/7 fl oz tepid water

2 tbsp olive oil, plus extra for oiling

2 tbsp milk

40 g/1 1/2 oz drained sun-dried
   tomatoes in oil, roughly chopped,
   plus extra for topping if required

2 tbsp shredded fresh basil

To make the Italian sponge, sift the flour into a warmed bowl. Stir in the yeast. Make a well in the centre. Add the water and mix into the flour mixture. Cover with clingfilm and leave in a warm place overnight or for 12 hours.

To make the dough, sift the flour and salt together into a separate bowl. Stir in the yeast and sugar. Make a well in the centre. Add the water, oil and milk to the sponge mixture and mix together, then add to the well and mix to form a dough.

Turn out the dough on a lightly floured work surface and knead for 5-10 minutes, or until smooth and elastic. Knead in the sun-dried tomatoes and basil. Put the dough in a large bowl, cover with lightly oiled clingfilm and leave to rise in a warm place for 1 hour.

Lightly flour 2 baking sheets. Halve the dough, using a spoon, and gently tip each half onto a prepared baking sheet. Shape each piece into a rectangular loaf about 2.5 cm/1 inch thick. Dust with flour and leave, uncovered, to prove in a warm place for 30 minutes. Preheat the oven to 220°C/425°F/Gas Mark 7.

Scatter extra sun-dried tomatoes over the tops of the loaves, if you like. Bake in the preheated oven for 25-30 minutes until the loaves are golden. Transfer to a wire rack and leave to cool.

Ciabatta dough should be almost
batter-like and very sticky.

OLIVE BREAD

This olive-enriched bread is ideal to serve with starters, or to accompany soups. Choose either black or green olives, according to your preference.

Lightly oil a baking sheet. Sift the flour and salt together into a large bowl. Stir in the yeast, 2 teaspoons of the sesame seeds and the oregano. Make a well in the centre. Add the water and oil to the well and mix to form a firm dough.

Turn out the dough onto a lightly floured work surface and knead for 10 minutes, or until smooth and elastic. Put the dough in a bowl, cover with a clean, damp tea towel and leave to rise in a warm place for 1 hour, or until doubled in size.

Turn out again and knead lightly, then knead in the olives. Cut the dough in half and shape each half into a smooth round. Transfer to the prepared baking sheet, cover with a clean tea towel and leave to prove in a warm place for 30 minutes. Preheat the oven to 220°C/425°F/Gas Mark 7.

Using a sharp knife, make slashes across the top of each loaf. Lightly brush with oil and sprinkle with the remaining sesame seeds. Bake in the preheated oven for 10 minutes. Reduce the temperature to 190°C/375°F/Gas Mark 5. Bake for a further 25 minutes, or until golden and the loaves sound hollow when tapped on the base. Leave to cool on a wire rack.

MAKES 2 MEDIUM LOAVES

3 tbsp olive oil, plus extra for oiling and brushing

900 g/2 lb strong white bread flour, plus extra for dusting

1 tsp salt

1¹/2 tsp easy-blend dried yeast

3 tsp sesame seeds

¹/2 tsp dried oregano

600 ml/1 pint warm water

225 g/8 oz olives, stoned and roughly chopped

PITTA BREAD

Lightly oil a baking sheet.

Sift the flour and salt together into a warmed bowl. Stir in the yeast and sugar. Make a well in the centre. Add the water and oil to the well and mix to form a dough.

Turn out the dough onto a lightly floured work surface and knead for 5–10 minutes, or until smooth and elastic. Put the dough in an oiled bowl, cover with clingfilm and leave to rise in a warm place for 1 hour, or until doubled in size.

Turn out the dough again and knead lightly. Cut the dough into 6 equal pieces and shape each piece into a ball. Transfer to the prepared baking sheet. Cover with oiled clingfilm and leave to prove in a warm place for 10 minutes. Put 2–3 baking sheets in the oven and preheat the oven to 230°C/450°F/Gas Mark 8.

Flatten each piece of dough slightly, then roll out each piece into a round. Sprinkle lightly with flour and cover with clingfilm. Leave for 10 minutes to rest.

Transfer the dough rounds to the hot baking sheets, spaced well apart, and bake in the preheated oven for 5 minutes, or until risen and golden. Transfer to a wire rack and leave to cool.

MAKES 6

1 tbsp olive oil, plus extra for oiling

350 g/12 oz strong white bread flour, plus extra for dusting

$1^1/_2$ tsp salt

1 tsp easy-blend dried yeast

1 tsp sugar

210 ml/$7^1/_2$ fl oz tepid water

NAAN BREAD

These leavened breads have been baked in India since the days of Moghul rule, traditionally by slapping the rolled and shaped dough against the hot inside of a charcoal-heated tandoor oven. Without the benefit of a tandoor oven, you need to preheat your oven with a baking sheet inside to its highest setting in plenty of time.

MAKES 10

900 g/2 lb strong white bread flour

1 tbsp baking powder

1 tsp sugar

1 tsp salt

300 ml/10 fl oz water, heated to
   50°C/122°F

1 egg, beaten

55 g/2 oz ghee, melted, plus extra for
   rolling out and brushing

Sift the flour, baking powder, sugar and salt together into a large bowl. Make a well in the centre. Beat the water and egg together in a bowl. Gradually add to the well, using your fingers to draw in the flour from the side, until a stiff, heavy dough forms. Shape the dough into a ball and return it to the bowl.

Soak a clean tea towel in hot water, then wring it out and use it to cover the bowl, tucking the ends of the towel under the bowl. Leave to rest for 30 minutes.

Turn out the dough onto a work surface brushed with melted ghee and flatten the dough. Gradually sprinkle with the melted ghee and knead in, little by little. Shape the dough into 10 equal balls.

Resoak the towel in hot water and wring it out again, then place it over the dough balls. Leave to rise in a warm place for 1 hour. Put 1-2 baking sheets in the oven and preheat the oven to 230°C/450°F/Gas Mark 8 or its highest setting.

Use a lightly greased rolling pin to roll the dough balls into teardrop shapes, about 3 mm/$\frac{1}{8}$ inch thick. Lightly rub the hot baking sheets with ghee. Transfer the naans to the hot baking sheets and bake in the preheated oven for 5-6 minutes until golden brown and lightly puffed. Brush the hot naans with melted ghee and serve immediately.

CHAPATIS

MAKES 6

225 g/8 oz wholemeal flour, sifted, plus extra for dusting

1/2 tsp salt

150-200 ml/5-7 fl oz water

melted ghee, for brushing

This is the everyday bread for millions of Indians, eaten by virtually everyone from the richest to the very poor. The soft, malleable texture makes these flatbreads ideal for mopping up 'gravies', as Indian sauces are known, and for scooping up bite-sized portions of food, doing away with knives and forks. Unleavened chapatis are traditionally made with *atta*, a type of Indian wholemeal flour that is sold in Asian food shops and some large supermarkets, but ordinary wholemeal flour is fine if you sift out the gritty pieces of bran first.

Sift the flour and salt together into a large bowl. Make a well in the centre. Gradually stir in enough water to make a stiff dough.

Turn out the dough onto a lightly floured surface and knead for 10 minutes, or until smooth and elastic. Shape into a ball and put in a bowl. Cover with a damp tea towel and leave to rest for 20 minutes.

Cut the dough into 6 equal pieces. Lightly flour your hands and roll each piece into a ball. Heat a large, ungreased tava, frying pan or griddle over a high heat until very hot and a splash of water 'dances' when it hits the surface.

Working with one dough ball at a time, flatten, then roll out into an 18-cm/7-inch round. Add to the hot pan and cook until brown flecks appear on the bottom. Flip over and cook on the other side.

Flip the dough over again and use a bunched-up tea towel to press down all around the edge. This pushes the steam in the chapati around, causing the chapati to puff up. Continue cooking until the bottom is golden brown, then flip over and repeat on the other side.

Brush the chapati with melted ghee and serve. Repeat with the remaining dough balls. Chapatis are best served immediately, but they can be kept warm, wrapped in foil, for 20 minutes.

pies, savoury flans
AND *pizza*

Pies and flans know few boundaries: sweet or savoury, and baked in shortcrust, suet, choux or puff pastry. As well as the more traditional recipes such as Apple Pie and Fish Pie, here you will find more contemporary options such as Sweet Potato Pie and Key Lime Pie, and variations such as Peach Cobbler. The more adventurous pastry fan can try their hand at a Mushroom Gougère or a batch of Stilton and Walnut tartlets and to top it off, there are even recipes for that classic Italian dish, the pizza.

WENSLEYDALE APPLE PIE

Grease a 23-cm/9-inch round fluted tart tin.

Sift the flour and salt together into a bowl. Rub in the butter with your fingertips until the mixture resembles fine breadcrumbs. Rub in 100 g/3 1/2 oz grated Wensleydale cheese. Light beat the egg yolks and water together, then add to the mixture and mix to form a soft dough.

Turn out the dough onto a lightly floured work surface. Knead lightly until smooth. Wrap in foil or clingfilm and chill in the refrigerator for 30 minutes. Preheat the oven to 200ºC/400ºF/Gas Mark 6.

Roll out two-thirds of the pastry and use to line the prepared tin. Layer in the sliced apples with all but 1 teaspoon of the sugar and the spices.

Roll out the remaining pastry, dampen the edges of the pastry lining the tin and lay the rolled pastry on top. Press down well to seal the edges and cut away any excess pastry. Crimp the edges with the tines of a fork.

Beat the egg white in a small bowl and use to glaze the pie, sprinkling the remaining sugar over to give a crisp finish.

Bake in the preheated oven for 40-45 minutes until the pastry is crisp and golden.

Cut the pie into portions and slip a slice of cheese under the crust of each piece before serving.

SERVES 6-8

butter, for greasing

350 g/12 oz plain flour, plus extra
  for dusting

pinch of salt

100 g/3 1/2 oz butter, diced and chilled

100 g/3 1/2 oz Wensleydale cheese,
  grated

2 egg yolks

3 tbsp cold water

900 g/2 lb cooking apples, peeled,
  cored and thinly sliced

115 g/4 oz caster sugar

1/2 tsp ground cinnamon

1/2 tsp ground cloves

1 egg white

175 g/6 oz Wensleydale cheese, sliced,
  to serve

This recipe uses Wensleydale cheese in the pastry and also serves a little extra with
the hot pie so that it melts while being eaten. You will not need any cream.

KEY LIME PIE

SERVES 6-8

CRUMB CRUST

85 g/3 oz butter, melted, plus extra
  for greasing

175 g/6 oz digestive biscuits or
  ginger biscuits

2 tbsp caster sugar

1/2 tsp ground cinnamon

FILLING

400 ml/14 fl oz canned condensed milk

125 ml/4 fl oz freshly squeezed
  lime juice

finely grated rind of 3 limes

4 large egg yolks

freshly whipped cream, to serve

Preheat the oven to 160°C/325°F/
Gas Mark 3. Lightly grease a 23-
cm/9-inch round pie plate, about
4 cm/1¹/2 inches deep.

To make the crumb crust, put
the biscuits, sugar and cinnamon
into a food processor and process
until fine crumbs form - do not
overprocess to a powder. Add the butter and process again until the
crumbs are moistened.

Tip the crumb mixture into the pie plate and press over the base and
up the side. Transfer the pie plate to a baking sheet and bake in the
preheated oven for 5 minutes.

Meanwhile, beat the condensed milk, lime juice, lime rind, reserving
some for decorating, and egg yolks together in a bowl until well blended.

Remove the crumb crust from the oven, pour the filling into the
crumb crust and spread out to the edge. Bake for a further 15 minutes,
or until the filling is set around the edge but still wobbly in the centre.
Transfer to a wire rack and leave to cool completely, then cover and chill
in the refrigerator for at least 2 hours. Serve with dollops of whipped
cream and decorate with the reserved lime rind.

Tart and creamy, this classic American pie is ideal for summer
entertaining. Commercial key lime pies have green food colouring
added, but this recipe is undoctored and so has a pale cream colour.

SWEET POTATO PIE

To make the pastry, sift the flour, salt and sugar into a bowl. Rub in the butter and white vegetable fat with your fingertips until the mixture resembles fine breadcrumbs. Sprinkle over 2 tablespoons of the water and mix to form a soft dough. If the dough seems dry, add the extra 1/2 tablespoon water. Wrap in foil or clingfilm and chill in the refrigerator for at least 1 hour.

Meanwhile, to make the filling, bring a large saucepan of water to the boil over a high heat. Add the sweet potatoes and cook for 15 minutes. Drain, then cool under cold running water. When cool, peel, then mash. Put the sweet potatoes in a bowl and beat in the eggs and sugar until very smooth. Beat in the remaining ingredients, then cover and set aside until required.

When ready to bake, preheat the oven to 220°C/425°F/Gas Mark 7. Roll out the dough on a lightly floured work surface into a thin 28-cm/ 11-inch round and use to line a 23-cm/9-inch round pie plate, about 4 cm/1½ inches deep. Trim off the excess dough and press the floured tines of a fork around the edge.

Prick the base of the pastry case all over with the fork and put a piece of crumpled foil in the centre. Bake in the preheated oven for 12 minutes, or until lightly golden.

Remove the the foil, pour the filling into the pastry case and bake for a further 10 minutes. Reduce the temperature to 160°C/325°F/Gas Mark 3 and bake for a further 35 minutes, or until a knife inserted into the centre comes out clean. Transfer to a wire rack and leave to cool. Serve warm or at room temperature with whipped cream.

Serve slices of this pie and see if guests can guess the main ingredient – few people will expect the humble sweet potato to be turned into such a rich, indulgent dessert.

SERVES 8-10

PASTRY

175 g/6 oz plain flour, plus extra
for dusting

1/2 tsp salt

1/4 tsp caster sugar

40 g/1½ tbsp butter, diced and chilled

40 g/1½ oz white vegetable fat, diced
and chilled

2-2½ tbsp iced water

FILLING

500 g/1 lb 2 oz orange-fleshed
sweet potatoes, scrubbed

3 extra-large eggs, beaten

115 g/4 oz soft light brown sugar

350 ml/12 fl oz canned evaporated milk

40 g/1½ oz butter, melted

2 tsp vanilla extract

1 tsp ground cinnamon

1 tsp ground nutmeg or freshly
grated nutmeg

1/2 tsp salt

freshly whipped cream, to serve

FOREST FRUIT PIE

SERVES 4

FILLING

250 g/9 oz fresh blueberries

250 g/9 oz fresh raspberries

250 g/9 oz fresh blackberries

100 g/3^1/2 oz caster sugar

2 tbsp icing sugar, to decorate

whipped cream, to serve

PASTRY

200 g/7 oz plain flour, plus extra for
dusting

25 g/1 oz ground hazelnuts

100 g/3^1/2 oz unsalted butter, diced
and chilled, plus extra for greasing

finely grated rind of 1 lemon

1 egg yolk, beaten

4 tbsp milk

Pick over the berries and put in a saucepan with 3 tablespoons of the caster sugar and cook over a medium heat, stirring frequently, for 5 minutes. Remove from the heat.

To make the pastry, sieve the flour into a bowl, then stir in the hazelnuts. Rub in the butter with your fingertips until the mixture resembles breadcrumbs, then sieve in the remaining caster sugar. Add the lemon rind, egg yolk and 3 tablespoons of the milk and mix to form a dough. Turn out on to a lightly floured work surface and knead briefly. Wrap with clingfilm and chill in the refrigerator for 30 minutes.

Preheat the oven to 190ºC/375ºF/Gas Mark 5. Grease a 20-cm/8-inch pie dish with butter. Roll out two-thirds of the pastry to a thickness of 5 mm/^{1}/4 inch and use it to line the base and side of the dish. Spoon the berries into the pastry case. Brush the rim with water, then roll out the remaining pastry and use it to cover the pie. Trim and crimp round the edge, then make 2 small slits in the top and decorate with 2 leaf shapes cut out from the dough trimmings. Brush all over with the remaining milk. Bake in the preheated oven for 40 minutes.

Dust the pie with the icing sugar and serve with whipped cream.

RHUBARB CRUMBLE

Preheat the oven to 190ºC/375ºF/Gas Mark 5.

Cut the rhubarb into 2.5-cm/1-inch lengths and put in a 1.7-litre/3-pint ovenproof dish with the caster sugar and orange rind and juice.

To make the crumble, sift the flour into a bowl. Rub in the butter with your fingertips until the mixture resembles fine breadcrumbs. Stir in the brown sugar and ginger. Spread evenly over the fruit and press down lightly with a fork.

Transfer the dish to a baking sheet and bake in the centre of the preheated oven for 25-30 minutes until the crumble is golden brown.

Serve warm with cream, yogurt or custard.

SERVES 6

900 g/2 lb rhubarb

115 g/4 oz caster sugar

grated rind and juice of 1 orange

cream, yogurt or custard, to serve

CRUMBLE

225 g/8 oz plain white or
   wholemeal flour

115 g/4 oz butter, diced and chilled

115 g/4 oz soft light brown sugar

1 tsp ground ginger

Crumble is one of the simplest puddings, easy to make and delicious to eat. The first, forced shoots of rhubarb are the sweetest and the most tender. Ginger is often added to improve the flavour, but a little orange really adds to the taste. The crumble topping can be made with white or brown flour, and some nuts may be added, if you like.

PEACH COBBLER

Preheat the oven to 220°C/425°F/Gas Mark 7. Put the peaches in a 23-cm/9-inch square ovenproof dish that is also suitable for serving. Add the sugar, lemon juice, cornflour and almond essence and toss together. Bake the peaches in the preheated oven for 20 minutes.

Meanwhile, to make the topping, sift the flour, all but 2 tablespoons of the sugar, the baking powder and salt together into a bowl. Rub in the butter with your fingertips until the mixture resembles fine breadcrumbs. Mix the egg with 5 tablespoons of the milk in a jug, add to the mixture and mix with a fork to form a soft, sticky dough. If the dough seems dry, stir in the extra tablespoon of milk.

Reduce the oven temperature to 200°C/400°F/Gas Mark 6. Drop spoonfuls of the topping over the surface, without smoothing. Sprinkle

with the remaining sugar and bake for a further 15 minutes, or until the topping is golden brown and firm – the topping will spread as it cooks.

Serve the cobbler hot or at room temperature with ice cream on the side.

SERVES 6

6 peaches, peeled, stoned and sliced

4 tbsp caster sugar

1/2 tbsp lemon juice

1 1/2 tsp cornflour

1/2 tsp almond essence or vanilla extract

vanilla or pecan nut ice cream, to serve

COBBLER TOPPING

175 g/6 oz plain flour

115 g/4 oz caster sugar

1 1/2 tsp baking powder

1/2 tsp salt

85 g/3 oz butter, diced and chilled

1 egg

5-6 tbsp milk

Summertime in Georgia, in the southeastern US, means one thing – peaches, peaches and more peaches. This old-fashioned baked dessert with its 'cobblestone' topping is a traditional way to take advantage of the seasonal glut.

PEAR TART

SERVES 6

PASTRY

275 g/9^1/$_2$ oz plain flour

pinch of salt

125 g/4^1/$_2$ oz caster sugar

115 g/4 oz butter, cut into small pieces

1 egg

1 egg yolk

few drops vanilla essence

2-3 tsp water

sifted icing sugar, for sprinkling

FILLING

4 tbsp apricot jam

55 g/2 oz amaretti or ratafia biscuits, crumbled

850 g-1 kg/1 lb 14 oz-2 lb 4 oz pears, peeled and cored

1 tsp ground cinnamon

85 g/3 oz raisins

60 g/2^1/$_4$ oz soft light brown sugar

To make the pastry, sift the flour and salt onto a work surface, make a well in the centre and add the sugar, butter, egg, egg yolk, vanilla essence and most of the water.

Using the fingers, gradually work the flour into the other ingredients to form a smooth dough, adding more water if necessary. Wrap the dough and chill in the refrigerator for at least 1 hour.

Preheat the oven to 200°C/400°F/Gas Mark 6. Roll out three-quarters of the pastry and use to line a shallow 25-cm/10-inch cake tin or deep flan tin. To make the filling, spread the jam over the base and sprinkle with the biscuits.

Slice the pears very thinly. Arrange over the biscuits in the pastry case. Sprinkle with cinnamon, then with raisins and finally with brown sugar.

Roll out a thin sausage shape using one-third of the remaining pastry, and place around the edge of the pie. Roll the remainder into thin sausages and arrange in a lattice over the tart, 4 or 5 strips in each direction, attaching them to the strip around the edge.

Cook in the preheated oven for 50 minutes until golden brown and cooked through. Leave to cool, then serve the pie warm or chilled, sprinkled with sifted icing sugar.

Pears are a very popular fruit as part of a dessert. In this recipe they are flavoured with almonds, cinnamon, raisins and apricot jam. Choose ripe pears that are still firm. Don't peel and slice them in advance as the flesh will discolour and spoil the appearance of the tart.

FLAKY PASTRY FISH PIE

Preheat the oven to 200°C/400°F/Gas Mark 6. Grease a 1.2-litre/2-pint pie dish.

Put the fish in a frying pan and cover with the milk. Add the bay leaf, peppercorns and onion slices. Bring to the boil, then reduce the heat and simmer gently for 10-12 minutes.

Remove from the heat and pour off the milk into a measuring jug. Add a little extra milk if necessary to make the liquid up to 300 ml/10 fl oz. Flake the fish into large pieces, removing any bones.

Melt the butter in a saucepan over a low heat and add the flour. Cook, stirring constantly, for 2-3 minutes. Remove from the heat and gradually stir in the reserved milk, beating well after each addition. Return the saucepan to the heat and cook, stirring constantly, until thickened. Cook for a further 2-3 minutes until smooth and glossy. Season to taste with salt and pepper and stir in the parsley and cream.

Put the fish in the base of the prepared pie dish, then add the egg and season to taste with salt and pepper. Pour the sauce over the fish and mix gently.

Roll out the pastry on a lightly floured surface until just larger than the pie dish. Cut off a strip 1 cm/^{1}/$_2$ inch wide around the edge. Moisten the rim of the dish with water and press the pastry strip onto it. Moisten the pastry collar and put on the pastry lid. Crimp the edges firmly and glaze with the beaten egg. Garnish with the leftover pastry shaped into leaves, if you like.

Transfer the pie to a baking sheet and bake near the top of the preheated oven for 20-25 minutes. Cover with foil if getting too brown.

SERVES 4-6

40 g/1^1/$_2$ oz butter, plus extra for
   greasing

650 g/1 lb 7 oz white fish fillets,
   such as cod or haddock, skinned

300 ml/10 fl oz milk

1 bay leaf

4 peppercorns

1 small onion, finely sliced

40 g/1^1/$_2$ oz plain flour, plus extra
   for dusting

salt and pepper

1 tbsp chopped fresh parsley
   or tarragon

150 ml/5 fl oz single cream

2 hard-boiled eggs, roughly chopped

400 g/14 oz ready-made flaky pastry,
   thawed if frozen

1 egg, beaten

Creamy fish and flaky pastry is a marriage made in heaven. This recipe suggests using white fish fillets, but you can use other fish if you prefer - a mixture of haddock and smoked haddock is good.

MUSHROOM GOUGÈRE

SERVES 4

CHOUX PASTRY

55 g/2 oz butter, plus extra
   for greasing

70 g/2^{1}/$_{2}$ oz strong white bread flour

pinch of salt

150 ml/5 fl oz water

2 eggs

55 g/2 oz Emmenthal cheese, grated

FILLING

2 tbsp olive oil

1 onion, chopped

225 g/8 oz chestnut mushrooms,
   sliced

2 garlic cloves, finely chopped

1 tbsp plain flour

150 ml/5 fl oz vegetable stock

85 g/3 oz walnuts, chopped

2 tbsp chopped fresh parsley

salt and pepper

Preheat the oven to 200°C/400°F/Gas Mark 6. Grease a round ovenproof dish.

To make the pastry, sift the flour and salt together onto a sheet of greaseproof paper. Put the water and butter in a saucepan over a low heat and heat until the butter has melted. Bring to a rolling boil. Remove from the heat and add the flour, all at once, beating well until the mixture leaves the side of the saucepan and forms a ball. Leave to cool slightly. Gradually beat in the eggs until the dough is smooth and glossy. Beat in the cheese. Spoon the pastry around the side of the prepared dish.

To make the filling, heat the oil in a large, heavy-based frying pan over a medium heat. Add the onion and cook, stirring frequently, for 5 minutes, or until softened. Add the mushrooms and garlic and cook, stirring, for 2 minutes. Stir in the flour and cook, stirring constantly, for 1 minute. Gradually stir in the stock. Bring to the boil, stirring constantly, and cook for 3 minutes, or until thickened. Reserve 2 tablespoons of the walnuts. Stir the remainder into the mushroom mixture with the chopped parsley. Season to taste with salt and pepper.

Spoon the filling into the centre of the dish and sprinkle over the remaining walnuts. Bake in the preheated oven for 40 minutes, or until the pastry is risen and golden. Serve at once.

LEEK AND SPINACH PIE

SERVES 6-8

2 tbsp unsalted butter, plus extra for
   greasing
250 g/9 oz ready-made puff pastry,
   thawed if frozen
plain flour, for dusting
2 leeks, finely sliced
225 g/8 oz fresh spinach leaves,
   chopped
2 eggs
300 ml/10 fl oz double cream
pinch of dried thyme
salt and pepper

Grease a 20-cm/8-inch round fluted flan dish. Roll out the pastry on a lightly floured work surface and leave to rest for 5 minutes. Use to line the flan dish so that a little pastry overhangs evenly all round the edge. Cover and chill in the refrigerator while you make the filling.

Preheat the oven to 180°C/350°F/Gas Mark 4.

Melt the butter in a large frying pan over a medium heat. Add the leeks and cook, stirring frequently, for 5 minutes, or until softened. Add the spinach and cook for 3 minutes, stirring frequently, until wilted. Leave to cool.

Beat the eggs in a bowl. Stir in the cream, thyme and salt and pepper to taste. Spread the cooked vegetables over the base of the pastry case. Pour in the egg mixture.

Transfer the flan dish to a baking sheet and bake in the preheated oven for 30 minutes, or until set. Leave to rest for 10 minutes before serving. Serve directly from the flan dish.

TOMATO AND GRUYÈRE TART

Grease a 20-cm/8-inch round fluted flan dish. Sift the flour into a large bowl. Rub in the butter with your fingertips until the mixture resembles fine breadcrumbs. Add enough of the water to mix to a firm dough. Roll out on a lightly floured work surface and use to line. Prick the base of the pastry case all over with a fork and chill in the refrigerator for 1 hour.

Preheat the oven to 200°C/400°F/Gas Mark 6.

Heat the oil in a frying pan over a medium heat. Add the onions and cook, stirring frequently, for 10-15 minutes, or until browned. Meanwhile, put a piece of crumpled foil in the centre of the pastry case and bake in the preheated oven for 12 minutes. Remove the foil and bake for a further 5 minutes, or until just golden. Transfer the onions to the pastry case and scatter over the cheese. Arrange the tomatoes on top.

Beat the cream, eggs and chives together in a bowl. Season well with salt and pepper and pour into the pastry case.

Reduce the oven temperature to 180°C/350°F/Gas Mark 4 and bake the tart for 30-35 minutes until set and browned. Garnish with thyme sprigs and serve.

SERVES 6

115 g/4 oz butter or margarine, diced
and chilled, plus extra for greasing

225 g/8 oz plain flour, plus extra
for dusting

3-4 tbsp iced water

2 tbsp oil

2 onions, sliced

115 g/4 oz Gruyère cheese, grated

10 oven-dried tomato halves

300 ml/10 fl oz double cream

2 large eggs

handful of fresh chives, snipped

salt and pepper

few fresh thyme sprigs, to garnish

STILTON AND WALNUT TARTLETS

Lightly grease a 7.5-cm/3-inch 12-hole muffin tin. Sift the flour and the celery salt together into a food processor, add the butter and process until the mixture resembles fine breadcrumbs. Alternatively, rub the fat into the flour mixture in a bowl with your fingertips. Tip into a large bowl and add the walnuts and enough iced water to form a firm dough.

Turn out onto a lightly floured work surface and cut the dough in half. Roll out one half. Using a 9-cm/3^1/$_2$-inch pastry cutter, cut out 6 rounds. Roll out each round to 12 cm/4^1/$_2$ inches in diameter and use to line half the muffin holes. Repeat with the remaining dough. Line each hole with baking paper and fill with baking beans. Chill in the refrigerator for 30 minutes. Preheat the oven to 200°C/400°F/Gas Mark 6.

Bake the tartlet cases in the preheated oven for 10 minutes. Remove from the oven, then remove the paper and beans.

To make the filling, melt the butter in a frying pan over a medium-low heat. Add the celery and leek and cook, stirring occasionally, for 15 minutes until very soft. Add the 2 tablespoons cream, crumble in the cheese and mix well. Season to taste with salt and pepper. Put the remaining cream in a saucepan and bring to simmering point. Pour onto the egg yolks in a heatproof bowl, stirring constantly. Mix in the cheese mixture and spoon into the tartlet cases.

Bake for 10 minutes, then turn the tin around and bake for a further 5 minutes. Leave the tartlets to cool in the tin for 5 minutes. Serve garnished with parsley.

This is a good pastry for sweet or savoury dishes.
Hazelnuts and pecans also work well but do not overchop the nuts; they should only be chopped finely enough to combine well with the pastry.

MAKES 12

WALNUT PASTRY
100 g/3^1/$_2$ oz butter, diced and chilled,
   plus extra for greasing
225 g/8 oz plain flour, plus extra
   for dusting
pinch of celery salt
25 g/1 oz walnut halves, chopped

FILLING
25 g/1 oz butter
2 celery sticks, finely chopped
1 small leek, finely chopped
200 ml/7 fl oz double cream,
   plus 2 tbsp
200 g/7 oz Stilton cheese
3 egg yolks
salt and pepper
chopped fresh flat-leaf parsley and
   parsley sprigs, to garnish

SPRING VEGETABLE TART

SERVES 4

PASTRY

125 g/4¹/₂ oz butter, diced and chilled,
  plus extra for greasing

250 g/9 oz plain flour, plus extra
  for dusting

pinch of salt

50 g/1³/₄ oz freshly grated
  Parmesan cheese

1 egg

FILLING

300 g/10¹/₂ oz mixed baby spring
  vegetables, such as carrots,
  asparagus, peas, broad beans, salad
  onions, sweetcorn and leeks

300 ml/10 fl oz double cream

125 g/4¹/₂ oz mature Cheddar cheese,
  grated

2 eggs, plus 3 egg yolks

handful of fresh tarragon and flat-leaf
  parsley, chopped

salt and pepper

Grease a 25-cm/10-inch round loose-based tart tin. Sift the flour and the salt together into a food processor, add the butter and process until the mixture resembles fine breadcrumbs. Alternatively, rub the fat into the flour mixture in a bowl with your fingertips. Tip into a large bowl and stir in the Parmesan cheese. Beat the egg and a little iced water together in a small bowl. Add most of the egg mixture and mix to form a soft dough, adding more if necessary.

Turn out onto a lightly floured work surface. Roll out into a round 8 cm/3¹/₄ inches larger than the tin and use to line the tin. Roll the rolling pin over the tin to neaten and trim the edge. Line the tart case with baking paper and fill with baking beans. Chill in the refrigerator for 30 minutes. Preheat the oven to 200°C/400°F/Gas Mark 6.

Bake the tart case in the preheated oven for 15 minutes. Remove the paper and beans and bake for a further 5 minutes. Remove from the oven and leave to cool. Reduce the oven temperature to 180°C/350°F/Gas Mark 4.

Prepare the vegetables as necessary, then cut into bite-sized pieces. Bring a large saucepan of lightly salted water to the boil. Add the vegetables and blanch for 2 minutes. Drain and leave to cool. Put the cream in a separate saucepan and bring to simmering point. Put the Cheddar cheese, eggs and egg yolks in a heatproof bowl and pour over the hot cream. Add the herbs and salt and pepper to taste and stir to combine. Arrange the vegetables in the tart case, pour over the cheese custard and bake for 30-40 minutes until just set. Leave to cool in the tin for 10 minutes before serving.

Use only the most tender young vegetables for this tart. If they are really small, you can leave them whole. A few slices of soft goat's cheese can be added just before baking.

FOUR SEASONS PIZZA

MAKES 2 X 15-CM/6-INCH PIZZAS

oil for oiling

250 g/9 oz ready pizza dough mix

TOMATO SAUCE

2 tbsp olive oil

1 small onion, finely chopped

1 garlic clove, finely chopped

1 red pepper, deseeded and chopped

225 g/8 oz plum tomatoes, peeled
    and chopped

1 tbsp tomato purée

1 tsp soft light brown sugar

1 tbsp shredded fresh basil leaves

1 bay leaf

salt and pepper

TOPPING

70 g/2^1/2 oz canned or bottled anchovy
    fillets, drained and halved lengthways

55 g/2 oz artichoke hearts, thinly sliced

25 g/1 oz mozzarella cheese, thinly
    sliced

1 tomato, thinly sliced

100 g/3^1/2 oz mushrooms, thinly sliced

2 tsp capers, rinsed

2 tsp stoned, sliced black olives

2 tbsp olive oil

salt and pepper

Lightly oil a baking sheet. To make the tomato sauce, heat the oil in a heavy-based saucepan over a low heat. Add the onion, garlic and red pepper and cook, stirring occasionally, for 5 minutes, or until softened. Add the tomatoes, tomato purée, sugar, basil and bay leaf and season to taste with salt and pepper. Cover and simmer, stirring occasionally, for 30 minutes. Remove from the heat and leave to cool completely.

Make up the dough according to the packet instructions. Once risen, shape into 2 equal rounds about 5 mm/^{1}/4 inch thick. Transfer to the prepared baking sheet, cover with clingfilm and leave to rise in a warm place for 20-30 minutes. Preheat the oven to 200°C/400°F/Gas Mark 6.

Spread the tomato sauce over the pizza bases, almost to the edge. Cover one quarter with anchovy fillets. Cover a second quarter with sliced artichoke hearts. Cover the third quarter with alternate slices of mozzarella cheese and tomato. Cover the final quarter with sliced mushrooms. Scatter with the capers and olives, season to taste with salt and pepper and drizzle with oil. Bake in the preheated oven for 15-20 minutes, or until the cheese has browned and the bases have risen.

TOMATO AND PEPPERONI PIZZA

MAKES 4 X 15-CM/ 6-INCH PIZZAS

1 tbsp olive oil, plus extra for oiling

500 g/1 lb 2 oz ready-to-make
    pizza dough mix

2 tbsp green pesto

2 onions, sliced

55 g/2 oz pepperoni slices

150 g/5 1/2 oz mozzarella cheese, torn
    into pieces

225 g/8 oz cherry tomatoes, halved

12 olives

few fresh basil leaves

pepper

mixed salad, to serve

Lightly oil a large baking sheet.

Make up the dough according to the packet instructions. Once risen, shape into 4 equal rounds about 5 mm/1/4 inch thick. Transfer to the prepared baking sheet, cover with clingfilm and leave to rise in a warm place for 20-30 minutes. Preheat the oven to 200°C/400°F/Gas Mark 6.

Spread the pesto over the pizza bases, almost to the edge. Heat the oil in a large frying pan over a medium heat. Add the onions and cook, stirring frequently, for 3-4 minutes until softened. Scatter over the pizza bases. Arrange the pepperoni and cheese slices on top, then tuck in the cherry tomato halves. Scatter the olives and basil over the top and season well with pepper.

Bake the pizzas in the preheated oven for 15-20 minutes, or until the cheese has browned and the bases have risen. Serve immediately with a mixed salad.

INDEX